Bromley
In The Front Line

LEWIS BLAKE

The story of the London Borough of Bromley
under enemy attack in the Second World War,
told principally from official war records.

THE LONDON BOROUGH

BROMLEY LIBRARIES 2005

FIRST PUBLISHED BY THE AUTHOR 1980
REPRNTED 1981

SECOND EDITION 1983
REPRINTED WITH NEW COVER 1988

THIRD EDITION PUBLISHED 2005
by
Bromley Libraries
Central Library
High Street
Bromley BR1 1EX
020 8460 9955

ISBN 0 9010002 19 4

Printed by Antony Rowe

CONTENTS

GLOSSARY

AA	Anti-aircraft (guns)
AB500/1000	Canisters containing hundreds of IBs
Ack Ack	Anti-aircraft gunfire
AFS	Auxiliary Fire Service
ARP	Air Raid Precautions
ATS	(Women's) Auxiliary Territorial Service
C50	50kg IB with explosive charge
CD	Civil Defence (formerly ARP)
D/A	Delay action (fuse)
D/H	Direct Hit
Diver	Defensive arrangements against VI flying bombs
Do17/Do217	Dornier bombers
FAP	First Aid Post
FW190	Focke-Wulf fighter/ fighter-bomber
GAF	German Air Force/ Luftwaffe
HAA	Heavy anti-aircraft (guns)
HE	High Explosive/ High Explosive bomb
He111	Heinkel 111 bomber
HG	Home Guard
IAZ	Inner Artillery Zone
IB	Incendiary bomb
Iben/Ibsen	Explosive IB/ Separating explosive IB
Ju88/ 188	Junkers bombers
LAA	Light anti-aircraft (guns)
LCC	London County Council
LFB	London Fire Brigade
LRR	Long range rocket (V2)
Me109/Bf 109	Messerschmitt single engine fighter
Me110	" fighter bomber/medium bomber
Me410	" fast bomber
MG	Machine gun
MPI	Mean Point of Impact
NFS	National Fire Service
OB	Oil Bomb
PhIB	Phosphorous bomb
POI	Point of Impact
ROC	Royal Observer Corps
UP	Un-rotated projectile (AA rocket)
UX	Unexploded
UXB	Unexploded Bomb
VI	German flying bomb
V2	German long-range rocket
WRNS	Women's Royal Naval Service (Wrens)
WAAF	Women's Auxiliary Air Force
W/T	Wireless transmitter

1) Dornier 17 shot down off Blackness Lane, Leaves Green, 18 August 1940. Crashed in flames after being hit by AA fire at Kenley and by machine gun fire from pursuing Hurricane fighters. (Imperial War Museum)

INTRODUCTION

The first identified air raid incident in the Bromley area occurred on the night of 30 July 1940. A 'stick' of HEs came down near Stagmanspit Cottages, Layhams Road, Keston, without warning, causing some slight damage but no casualties. Bromley's last recorded incident and almost the last anywhere in Britain - certainly the last of any consequence - was a VI flying bomb at Scadbury Park, Chislehurst at breakfast time, 28 March 1945. Twelve hours earlier, the final V2 rocket to descend on Britain struck Court Road/ Kynaston Road, Orpington.

The first event - in Layhams Road - involved 50kg bombs carried by a piloted aircraft travelling at around 240mph. The penultimate incident, less than five years later, concerned a long-range missile launched from Holland, armed with a one ton warhead and arriving at about four times the speed of sound. In terms of military technology the two occurrences belonged to different eras. In between, the Bromley area sustained frequent and prolonged attacks with HE bombs of increasing power, parachute mines, incendiary bombs, oil bombs, phosphorous bombs, VIs, V2s, sometimes cannon and machine gun fire - not to mention 'friendly' fire from errant anti-aircraft shells and rockets.

Most attacks were part of the general bombardment of London, or an overspill from the bombing of Biggin Hill airfield and dogfights between the RAF and the *Luftwaffe* during the Battle of Britain. Occasionally - the night of 16-17 April 1941 stands out particularly - the Bromley area appears to have been selected as an aiming point in its own right.

The following pages provide an account of what happened in the boroughs that were later incorporated into the London Borough of Bromley, from the first bombs at Keston to the convulsions of a dying tyranny represented here in SE England by flying bombs and rockets. Sidcup and Knockholt also receive coverage, because they were part of the original boroughs, although not taken into Bromley in the 1965 local government re-organisation. To avoid confusion, I have considered it best to use the term 'Bromley area' or 'Bromley district' when referring to the old local authority areas as a whole or some unspecified part of them.

When it first appeared 25 years ago, *Bromley In The Front Line* was believed to be unique in giving a detailed, factual coverage of air attacks in the Second

World War on a specific suburban area of London, dealing with the whole period during which London was under attack. Most of the material had not been published before. But much happens in a quarter of a century. Much more becomes known. More light is thrown on what were thought to be the facts. All of which has invited changes and updating in this edition, and the opportunity has been taken to make substantial revisions and to eliminate earlier printers' errors.

As before, the incidents, events, and descriptions are treated from a civilian standpoint. The book is not presented as a military history or that of any particular branch of the Home Front. However, more is done this time to put local events in the broader context of the air war in order that the interested reader may see them in better perspective.

I should like to thank London Borough of Bromley, Education and Libraries Directorate, for making this edition possible, and in particular Simon Finch and the staff of Bromley Local Studies Library for present and past help in the researches and in the publishing process. A note of grateful appreciation is extended for the assistance of the Public Record Office (now the National Archives), Guildhall Library, Imperial War Museum, London Metropolitan Archives, Lewisham Local Studies Centre, and Kent County Archives.

Many private people have generously contributed material and memories. Not all are mentioned by name in the text. Whether named or not, their contributions have proved invaluable for both authentic, contemporary colour and factual reality, and for that I thank them sincerely. Thanks are also due to my son, Lewis, whose training in aeronautical engineering, experience as a commercial pilot, and, not least, his expertise in the arcane workings of computers have been a constant source of support and guidance.

Over 7,000 people - men, women, and children - were killed or injured in air attacks within the area of today's London Borough of Bromley, plus Sidcup and Knockholt. There were other local people who suffered likewise while outside the area, and those injured who went unrecorded in the official returns. To all these, the dead and the surviving, I dedicate this book in the hope that it will serve as a small tribute to the sacrifices of a past civilian generation, whose like we shall not see again.

Lewis Blake, Bromley, February 2005

CHAPTER I

The Battle of Britain Comes to Bromley

This animal is very mischievous; when attacked it defends itself.
(La Menagerie)

London's first direct taste of the Battle of Britain came on the evening of Thursday, 15 August 1940. Whether intentionally or in mistake for RAF Kenley, a force of Me110 fighter-bombers delivered a savage attack on Croydon aerodrome and on factories at an adjoining industrial estate. There was no raid warning beforehand. This came only after the raiders had left the scene of their handiwork: buildings demolished or on fire, still and silent bodies on the ground, people streaming blood, hobbling to the aid of those with more serious injuries. Nemesis in the shape of RAF fighters caught up with some of the raiders, including their leader and the group adjutant - both killed.

Numerous people in the Bromley area were puzzled spectators of this episode, in which 63 civilians were killed and 285 injured, plus a number of RAF personnel. They stood on street corners and at garden gates watching and pointing to puffs of smoke in the sky and aircraft in line making shallow dives before disappearing from view behind the Shirley Hills. Their mystification was due to the absence of warning from the sirens, leaving them unsure whether they were seeing a real air raid or a rather realistic exercise of some sort. The belated alert settled all doubts and most then hastened to take cover.

Henceforth in that summer and autumn, no day passed without one or more air raid alerts; sometimes as many as six in a day, making it almost impossible to carry on the normal routines of daily life - cooking, shopping, sitting down to regular meals, travelling, even taking a bath.

The King's Arms at Leaves Green lay uncomfortably close to the main runway of RAF Biggin Hill. Small wonder that off-duty fighter pilots preferred to drive over to The White Hart at Brasted! Most patrons at lunchtime Sunday, 18 August were aware, without allowing it to disturb their Sabbath drinking, that sooner or later visits from the Luftwaffe were inevitable. Just how soon they were about to find out.

When the sirens went at 1.20pm a number in an expansive frame of mind ventured into the forecourt, not wishing to miss any excitement, and doubtless prepared to offer one another the benefit of their views on how the expected battle should be conducted. Moments later MG and cannon fire

2) Biggin Hill air raid siren. Apart from a few false alarms, this siren first sounded 'in earnest' on the evening of 15 August 1940 for a raid on Croydon airfield. It blared forth its undulating warning sound for the first attack on RAF Biggin Hill on Sunday 18 August. After that like all the sirens in the London area it was seldom silent for long (Lewis Blake).

swept the pub as a low-flying and burning Dornier exchanged shots with a Hurricane fighter in hot pursuit. Fourteen people near the pub were reported injured; whether from these flying bullets or from high level bombing by Heinkel IIIs which followed is not clear.

The burning Dornier ended its inglorious flight with a belly-landing in a field off Blackness Lane, one mile north of the pub. It had just taken part in a low-level attack on RAF Kenley, having then been damaged by light AA fire, chased by Hurricanes in a running battle across country, and received a fusillade of rifle shots from Addington Home Guard. It was lucky not to have performed a spectacular encore by colliding with high voltage cables of the National Grid, which cross the field where it crashed. Although the crew escaped with their lives, they next had to throw themselves in a ditch with their British captors as bombs from their own side began to rain down on Biggin Hill airfield. Early reports of their deaths were clearly exaggerated!

The Dornier's destruction was popularly - and officially - attributed to Addington Home Guard, mainly to settle competing claims between RAF pilots and Bofors gunners at Kenley, and to give 'Dad's Army' a morale boost and show it was now a real force in the defence of the country. The national Press seized on the story and gave it the widest publicity of any single German aircraft destroyed in the Battle of Britain. A War Office statement said, "... during air raids on Sunday a few Home Guard in the south London area were attacked by machine gun fire... They retaliated with rifle fire and after firing 180 rounds caused the enemy aircraft to crash."

Back at the The King's Arms several cars in the forecourt were set alight and burnt out, despite the early arrival of fire appliances from Biggin Hill village, which used water from a nearby pond to tackle the flames. A Chislehurst man out for a Sunday drive in his car finished his trip in an ambulance after being hit in the thigh by a bomb splinter when he went to aid the injured. Heavy bombing of the airfield led to at least six civilian deaths in Leaves Green - two died at 3 Leaves Green Crescent and four in their garden Anderson shelter.

Altogether, 80 HE bombs were reported as having missed the airfield - seven on Downe golf course which injured six people (a golfer was also hit in the foot by a machine gun bullet); 32 in Main Road and New Year's Lane, Knockholt, with casualties reported at Lower Petleys and Homefield House; four at Luxted, damaging Bird House camp; 30 fairly harmlessly at Cudham; and several in Jail Lane and Christy Road, Biggin Hill, where one person was reported killed at the Old Jail Inn.

Up to 400 bombs were recorded on the airfield itself. Nothing of vital importance was seriously damaged on this occasion. The runways were heavily cratered, but this was rectified fairly quickly while markers were placed to show pilots clear areas suitable for a safe touch-down.

Mrs Kennedy at Addington Village recorded in her diary: "1.10 - 2.10pm. Dreadful raid here. Absolute Bedlam. Planes hedgehopping everywhere. Another raid 5.40 - 6.15pm. Not here."

Violet Tyler in Lewisham recorded: "Another hot day. We were going to the zoo (Regents Park) and about to get on a 36 bus when the sirens went, so came back home. All Clear at 2pm. So off we went again. Got there at 3.30pm. Another warning at 5.40 - 6.10pm. Had to leave the zoo at 6.30pm. Terrible job to get a bus. Home at 8.30pm."

Following the first bombing of central London on 24-25 August 1940 - usually put down to navigational error by a couple of German crews participating in a raid on targets along the Thames Estuary - the Bromley area found itself under air raid alert on most nights, as well as during the day. The warning system was still having teething troubles. On the very next night, shortly after the All Clear sounded at 1.10am, a string of HEs fell across Bellingham Estate and Lower Sydenham, with the last one blowing out the backs of houses at the junction of Lennard Road and Kent House Road in Beckenham. One householder said, "The ARP arrived before the dust had properly settled". Their prompt arrival may have had something to do with their Post being only 200 yards away in Holy Trinity church hall!

Orpington control room knew before the phones began ringing frantically that RAF Biggin Hill was under heavy attack again. It was Friday evening, 30 August; the wall timepiece registered six o'clock. Twice already this day the airfield had faced raiders. Now the sound of distant explosions, the rattle of machine gun and cannon fire, and the quick bark of AA guns preceded first reports from wardens' posts of 'incidents' - a nice, neutral word often concealing something very nasty indeed.

The outbreak of serious fires at the fighter station and reports of heavy casualties following a direct hit on a trench shelter led to urgent requests for outside help. A score of fire appliances rushed to the airfield from Orpington, Bromley, Bexley, Chislehurst, and Westerham, avoiding craters and burst water mains en route in Westerham Road. Rescue and medical teams assisted in the grim task of recovering 39 bodies and rescuing 26 injured persons from the collapsed trench shelter. Most casualties were young women of the WAAFs (Women's Auxiliary Air Force), but eleven civilian workers were counted among the dead.

Stores, workshops, barracks, hangers, the armoury, and the guard room sustained hits from 500kg HEs. Power, gas, and water mains were broken, and all telephone lines to the north were put out of action. Two Me109 fighter escorts collided in mid-air at about this period, one crashing at Layhams Farm, West Wickham, the other at Fickleshole Farm, Chelsham. Neither German pilot survived.

Attacks resumed after dark between 9.20pm and 3.55am. Luxted and Berry's Green reported fifteen HEs, with houses on fire. Hundreds of IBs affected Knockholt, Cudham, and Biggin Hill village, where cottages in Coronation Terrace, Westerham Road were set alight. At 78 Clock House Road, Beckenham a husband and wife lost their lives to a 250kg HE, and in Franklin Road, Penge incendiaries set fire to the Co-op store.

Saturday brought no relief to Biggin Hill. Sirens wailed intermittently throughout the day, with all London Region placed under alert each time raiders approached RAF airfields along its southern perimeter. Soon after noon Biggin Hill came under high altitude bombing, causing further extensive damage to hangers, married quarters, the officers' mess, and the operations building, which took a direct hit and caught fire. Once more power and phone links were disrupted.

On Sunday morning Fighter Command's most battered airfield received its sixth raid in three days. Then at about 6pm a formation of Dorniers delivered a temporary coup de grâce by knocking out the sector operations room. All lines of communication (except one) to Fighter Command, airfields under Biggin Hill's control, and Observer Corps centres and posts were out of action. Post Office engineers worked tirelessly to restore services, even while the airfield was under attack. But for a time control passed to RAF Hornchurch. Later the property known as Towerfields near Keston ponds served as a temporary operations centre. Some reports also refer to a shop in Biggin Hill village used for this purpose.

Orpington Hospital suffered direct hits in which the boiler house and nurses' quarters were badly damaged. Five people were injured in King's Road, Orpington, and several HEs fell in the grounds of St Joseph's Orphanage in Sevenoaks Road. In the small back garden of their cottage, St Fillans in Orchard Road, Farnborough Village, the Lawrence family dutifully took to the Anderson shelter as aerial combats swirled overhead. While Percy Lawrence, his wife Phyllis, and their sons, John and David, aged eight and five, waited for the danger to pass, it may be supposed that they chatted amiably to divert their thoughts from more unpleasant matters. But fortune did not smile on them - all died when a bomb blasted the shelter out of the ground.

Blazing testimony to the intensity of these air battles could be seen in the burnt-out wreckage of many crashed aircraft in the outer suburbs. They included a Hurricane of 253 Squadron which crashed at Mace Farm, Cudham, the pilot having baled out, badly burned; a Spitfire reported crashed in Repository Road, Woolwich, near the Royal Artillery Barracks; a German bomber shot down near Overshaws, Cudham Lane; an Me109 shot down by Sgt. J. Stokoe, 603 Squadron, at Plumstead - it plunged into back gardens of terraced houses, with one wing gone and burning wreckage and exploding ammunition trapping people in their Anderson shelters; Hurricane crashes in the vicinity of Court Road, Orpington and another shot down over Kenley (pilot killed when parachute failed to open); an Me109 at Hurst Farm, Chilham (overturned and burst into flames); and an Me110 at Hosey Wood, Brasted.

There was little question but that the *Luftwaffe* were stepping up their night incursions over London from the beginning of September 1940. On the night of 5-6 September widespread damage occurred across SE London. Bromley was affected by fires among several High Street stores soon after midnight; the town reported 48 fires all told in the central area. At Petts Wood, a stick of HEs struck Willett Way, Sandhurst Road, and Haileybury Road. Three people lost their lives at 101 Bourne Way, Hayes.

Following four periods under alert during the day, due once more to attempts to bomb Biggin Hill, there were two air raids on the night of 6-7 September. The first lasted two and a half hours from 9pm. If people retired to bed when the All Clear sounded at 11.30pm, they were probably still awake when the sirens called them up again at midnight. It would be 4am before the next All Clear. No bombing appears to have involved Bromley directly. In the Blitz, however, a whole night's rest could be lost without hearing a single bomb explode. Heavy AA gunfire from every quarter would see to that, as might ever-present tenseness and anxious anticipation of what might happen next.

Heavy Ack-Ack (HAA) gun-sites close enough to Bromley to make their presence strongly felt included Hayes Common, Shirley Park, St Paul's Cray, Bickley (Thornet Wood), Beckenham (Elgood Playing Field), Anerley (rear of town hall), Beckenham Place Park (two sites; one at Summerhouse Hill), Sundridge Park, Grove Park, and Dulwich Park. A mix of 4.5 inch, the latest 3.7 inch, and First World War 3 inch, these guns, when fully engaging the enemy, pounded the sky and earth until buildings for miles around shook to their very foundations.

The people of Bromley were shocked spectators of the massive daylight attack on London's riverside boroughs on Saturday, 7 September. They witnessed with awe the mounting columns of black and grey smoke, constantly lit up by explosions, as thunderclouds are illuminated by split-second lightning. The more prudent kept under cover, for large-scale aerial battles spread across the suburbs once the RAF realised London was the target this time, not their own airfields.

Shoppers in local high streets were nearing completion of their weekend purchases when the raid started at 4.30pm. Between then and the time the last raiders left for home at 6.15pm wave after wave had set the northern horizon ablaze. With the fading of evening light, the sky above the Thames glowed an ever-deepening crimson, to become a fiery beacon visible for fifty miles around. And as a beacon it was used by the German crews when they came back to the target at about 8.30pm for a night of renewed bombing, "like a dog returning to its vomit", as one commentator put it.

Viewed from suburban Bromley the unfolding drama looked like Armageddon - with the forces of evil having the best of it. Intense sympathy for those who must be enduring sheer hell was tempered - not unnaturally - by apprehension of the bombardment spreading outwards to engulf their own neighbourhoods. Yet when the All Clear sounded just before 5am on Sunday only a handful of incidents had occurred locally. Eleven deaths were reported near Beckenham, including four elderly residents of Newlands Park Nursing Home, and in Bromley two were reported killed at 34 Alexandra Crescent.

The account would not be complete without mention of the bravery of Albert Dolphin, who lived at 21 Boyland Road, on the Bromley-Downham border. Employed as a porter at the South Eastern Hospital (later New Cross Hospital), he was on duty at 10.30pm when two wards and the nurses' quarters were severely damaged by a direct hit. Four nurses were killed instantly, and another lay trapped after she had been swept down to the ground floor by the collapse of the floor above. Albert Dolphin struggled to release her though aware that an adjacent wall was likely to fall at any moment. Minutes later it started to cave in, bringing down the shattered roof and other debris. The porter flung himself across the nurse's inert body and perished taking the full force of a cascade of masonry. The nurse survived, though injured, and for his supreme sacrifice a posthumous George Cross was awarded to Mr Dolphin, a very rare distinction even in the Blitz.

It was on the third anniversary of their daughter's death that Mrs Dolphin received the news of her loss. Many months passed before she could bring herself to tell her other daughter, aged seven and evacuated, that her father was also now dead.

Sunday, 15 September 1940 - a Sabbath forever remembered as Battle of Britain Day. On this date the climax and turning point in the fight for mastery of England's skies arrived. Now was the historic moment when The Few gained immortality in what was, without doubt, a modern Agincourt, watched by non-combatants who yet shared some of the dangers of the fight. Whether they, in the Bard's words, would have considered themselves accursed had they not been there is another matter.

By 2.30pm many an Olde English roast languished in the oven while families languished in cellars, garden shelters, and under stairs in hallways, waiting for the gladiatorial contests above their heads to exhaust themselves. Others stood in their gardens or in the streets, eyes riveted where the contrails of whirling aircraft drew intricate patterns in the Indian summer sky.

Before lunch 250 Dorniers and Me109 escorts crossed the Kent coast to be met by a swarm of Spitfires over the Weald. A gigantic battle developed with the aerial armada advancing on London, for since 7 September the Luftwaffe had switched its main effort from airfields to the capital. The battle spread out in a twisting whirlwind of individual combats five or six miles high, which sometimes swept as low as a few hundred feet. Squadrons of Hurricanes joined the fray over north west Kent and London's southern outskirts. When the tumult burst upon the suburbs over half the bombers had gone missing - shot down, damaged, chased all over the Home Counties, or simply running for home. The rest faced the guns of London's Inner Artillery Zone, the lurking balloon barrage, and yet more lethal encounters with the RAF.

After lunch it all happened again. The same pattern. The enemy in same strength. Only this time the RAF really excelled itself by sending up 21 fighter squadrons - nearly 200 aircraft - to confront and confound the intruders. There was no let up for anybody, up there or down on the ground, in this make-or-break day which would decide whether Germany persisted in its daylight onslaughts prior to invasion, or call the whole thing off while it considered its next moves.

Over SE London the German attack faltered and broke up in a fury of AA shells and air battles. Some bombers jettisoned their bombs and fled. The following were some of the consequences of their actions in the Bromley area:

Penge: Bourdon Road: One killed, eight injured at No. 23,
Queen Adelaide Road: One killed, six injured at No. 16,
St John's Road: Three killed, nine injured at No. 8,
Penge West Station blocked by unexploded bombs (UXB),
Oakfield Road: First Aid Post. Many casualties treated in the afternoon; the oldest, a woman of 78, badly bruised and in shock; the youngest, a baby girl of 2 years with head wounds; others had cut legs and arms, multiple abrasions, back injuries. one was treated for hysteria.
Beckenham: Crystal Palace Park Rd: 12 killed, including residents of No. 19 (Parklands Nursing Home); others died at No. 45, including Andrew Dick, MPS, a native of the Isle of Man.
Venner Road: Three killed at No. 222.
King's Hall Road: Three killed at No. 65.
Electricity station hit by HE.
Hayes: The New Inn, Station Approach: D/H. Virtually demolished. Two killed, Fred Scates and Charles Hammond. Rex Cinema badly damaged by blast from a second HE.
Orpington: Struck by 64 HEs, oil bombs, and 1,500 incendiaries during day and next night.
Petts Wood: HEs and IBs in Transmere Road, Brookmead Way, Tudor Way, Queensway, etc. One person killed, two injured.
Addington: Lodge Lane. Spitfire crashed in meadow. Pilot killed.
Biggin Hill: Me 109 shot down at Norheads Farm.
Barnehurst: Do17 shot down at Perry Street. Blew up on the ground.
Woolwich Arsenal: He111 bomber shot down and exploded among shell-

filling sheds.

The roaring and screaming of engines of aircraft engaged in low-level combat, interspersed with stuttering bursts of MG fire, and accompanied by the crash and shudder of bombs and guns, fed fear into those who sheltered and listened but for sight had only a feverish imagination for a window on the battle. Excitement rather than fear would have served eyewitnesses to the burning Dornier being repeatedly attacked by RAF fighters over Beckenham and Sydenham around mid-day. Had it just jettisoned bombs on Penge, killing or injuring 30 people? Some would have cheered when they saw two German crewmen bale out over Sydenham Wells Park and Dulwich. A third airman, badly wounded, landed by parachute at Kennington Oval and was allegedly set upon by an infuriated crowd. The Dornier, or what remained of it, finally crashed at Victoria Station.

As a general rule, censorship and the demands of security prevented the Press from divulging details of air raid incidents. This was especially restrictive and irksome for local newspapers, because without precision about time, place and people local reporting loses much of its point. Incidents - sometimes whole air raids - were ignored or occasionally described with much circumlocution. Small clues might be provided which were useful only to those who already had first-hand knowledge. (Space does not allow a fuller treatment here of the subtle nuances of British censorship in the war)

In security-conscious *Lewisham Borough News* the public house incident in Hayes was referred to in the following terms:

"The bomb which fell on the tavern killed the head waiter and the husband of one of the waitresses... The manager was injured... The inn was a large and high building of Cotswold stone in distinctive architecture and did not look like the conventional public house. It was built six or seven years ago on the site of an old fashioned red brick tavern, which had stood there for sixty years... Fred, the head waiter who was killed, was a favourite at the inn..."

And so on in similar vein for several paragraphs. No reference to the date or place is made. The item was opaque unless the reader happened to know Hayes well, which was not likely since Hayes was several miles outside the paper's circulation area. A similar report in the *Bromley and Kentish Times* offered a few more clues by saying the pub dominated a modern suburban high street with lock-up shops opposite, and that another bomb in the high street fell opposite a cinema.

Among the strangest missiles in the day's collection was an aluminium soapbox of German manufacture containing maggots in a greasy medium, which turned out to be a decomposed mouse. A Sidcup warden saw it drop. At the National Institute of Medical Research they identified the soap as made in Karlsruhe and not obtainable in Britain. The contents were described as offensive but harmless and dismissed as "in the nature of a practical joke". One can only feel a sneaking regard for the German flyer who found time for boyish jokes in the middle of a life and death struggle which might determine the course of the war.

Between the start of the great London Blitz on 7 September and the climax of the Battle of Britain on 15 September, all-night raids and large-scale attacks in daylight always involved Bromley, as one would expect from its location.

Incidents included houses destroyed in Oakfield Road, Penge, with six people killed and five injured. HEs in Southend Road, Beckenham (five deaths including a mother and two daughters, aged 9 and 3). D/A bombs at Flower House Estate, Southend Village, which exploded later and partly destroyed the lodge. HEs and IBs at Durham Hill and Moorside Road schools, Downham. Two people killed in West Wickham High Street, the roadway blocked by debris (night of 13-14th). Extensive fires in Anerley - Robin Hood garage, Crystal Palace Hotel, etc., one person killed and ten injured.

3) Among the first night incidents in Bromley was this at 128-130 Lennard Road, near junction with Kent House Road.

4) *Parklands Nursing Home at 19 Crystal Palace Park Road as it looked after a direct hit at the height of the Battle of Britain, 15 September 1940. Twelve people lost their lives here and at No. 45.*

5) *The New Inn, Station Approach, Hayes. Demolished by a direct hit during the air battles on 15 September 1940. The head waiter was killed on the spot and the husband of a waitress died of his injuries the following day.*

6) *Kenwood Court, Hayes Lane, Beckenham, bombed on 17 September 1940 with the loss of four lives: a widow and her two sons and an elderly lady, who may have been related.*

CHAPTER 2

Blitz Terror Weapon

And trust that out of night and death shall rise
The dawn of ampler life. (Sir Owen Seaman)

The all-night assault on the night of 17-18 September 1940 was of the kind Londoners were apt to call 'a bad raid'. All raids were bad. Some were worse than others. The thing which put this particular night in the latter category for SE London was the first use against civilians of the parachute mine - widely referred to as a landmine, to distinguish it from the almost identical weapon when used against shipping: the magnetic mine. It was still a misnomer, because landmines in military terms are buried in the ground. Calling it a parachute mine was an untidy compromise, for any mine sowed by aircraft came down by parachute.

Call it what you will, it became the most feared and most fearful of all weapons in the Blitz. Black cylinders, eight feet or six feet long and two feet in diameter, the mines contained one ton or half-ton of high explosive and were usually dropped in pairs by He111s. They fell noiselessly by parachute, so there was no audible warning of their descent. And because the gentle descent prevented ground penetration none of the blast was absorbed below the surface; it all went into smashing buildings over a wide radius. There was no pretence here of the mine being anything other than an indiscriminate terror weapon against civilian men, women, and children, for it was impossible to aim it with any degree of accuracy against legitimate war targets.

During the early use of the weapon SE London suburbs received the lion's share. The minelaying crews seemed definitely chary of flying into London's AA barrage, preferring instead to drop their weapons prematurely and turn back. The writer's surmise is that, because accustomed to sowing mines in estuaries and other shallow waters without much to fear from gunfire, they were easily unsettled by flak.

Of 40 mines dropped on London and the Home Counties on the first night, a half came down on SE London. In Bromley one pair descended on Tylney Road and at the rear of Widmore and Wanstead Roads. At least eight people lost their lives and 44 were injured; 60 homes were destroyed or severely damaged. Just after midnight Petts Wood was shaken by the explosion of a mine in Greenwood Close, which killed 8-year-old Michael Oliver at No.16 and injured six others. Six houses were destroyed and 320 damaged.

The soft landing of these missiles turned out a blessing in one respect, for it meant in the early days that about 30% failed to detonate. This was not so much a blessing for the Royal Navy officers who were called upon to defuse UX mines, risking their lives every time, nor in that UX mines caused large-scale evacuation and widespread disruption of transport and trade. The real benefit was that every UX specimen represented a saving in human life and in properties of all kinds, if successfully defused. Both Chislehurst and Sidcup had a UX mine to report on the first night - at Beavers Wood and Harland Avenue respectively.

On the next night, 18-19 September, about the same number of mines struck south eastern suburbs - again about half the national total. The worst incident locally was at St Mary Cray - a direct hit on the mansion known as East Hall. The mansion and adjoining cottages were destroyed by blast and fire, with ten lives lost and six people injured. Four mines fell on Bromley itself: at Homemead Avenue four persons were killed and 29 injured (26 houses destroyed or severely damaged). Near the junction of Glenview Road and Nightingale Lane, the Revd. Leslie Soul of St George's, Bickley was killed and 36 houses destroyed or badly damaged.

At Petts Wood mines killed three and injured four in Ladywood Avenue, and injured two in Towncourt Lane; a UX specimen at 185 The Avenue, West Wickham was safely defused by the Royal Navy; two more were dealt with in an orchard at the junction of Court Road/Warren Road, Orpington, and another in a field at Gray's Road, Cudham.

Incidents accumulated with every passing day, and with them the death-toll and injuries. Casualties on the 17-18th unconnected with mines included a widow and her two sons, and a woman of 86, killed at Kenwood Court, Hayes Lane, Beckenham. The remainder of September witnessed a dozen parachute mines in and around Bromley. On 19-20th a UX mine was caught up in branches of a tree at 7 Grosvenor Road, Orpington and later defused. Others exploded in woods near Locks Bottom (damaging West Kent Smallpox Hospital) and at Charmwood Farm, Pratts Bottom (farm buildings and 90 houses damaged).

Shortlands, Beckenham, Sidcup, and Keston were subject to mine attacks on 20-21 September. In Shortlands near the junction of Kingswood and Den roads there was one fatality and three injuries, with eight houses wrecked and 146 slightly damaged. St Mary's Church was also affected. In Beckenham the mine was a UX specimen in the garden of 55 The Avenue. It stopped all rail traffic through Beckenham Junction, making it a priority case for defusing. The Keston mine was also UX, in Cresswells Field, close to Downe Golf Course and half-mile NW of Downe Church. At Sidcup a pair fell at 9.30pm - one at Evans Nursery, Main Road, the other at Fisher's Farm, Main Road. Destruction was widespread: over 500 houses damaged, plus two pubs, three churches, a fire station, a laundry, garage, and council offices.

Over the next few nights significant incidents included a UX mine at 167 Longlands Road, Sidcup. Removed by the RN to a nearby field, it exploded a week later damaging nearly 300 houses. HEs were responsible for the destruction of 59 Cedars Road, Beckenham (two occupants killed); for two deaths at 24 Southbourne, Hayes; for three deaths at 36-38 Victor Road, Beckenham; and damage to Orpington's shopping centre.

During air battles a Spitfire was shot down and crashed into 70-72 Queensway, Coney Hall at 9.40am, 27 September. The pilot baled out but was found dead in Bourne Vale, Hayes. At 11.05am a Ju88 bomber was hit by AA fire and crashed in the grounds of Angus House, Cudham Lane. Three members of the crew baled out and were made prisoner; a fourth fell to his death due to parachute failure.

September ended with more large-scale attempts in daylight to attack Biggin Hill and Kenley airfields. One raid broke up in confusion over Knockholt and Westerham in a welter of surging air battles. The last night of the month produced fires and blast damage in Oak Grove Road and Croydon Road, Penge due to HE and oil bombs.

In Shortlands, a family of four were killed at 129 Queen Anne Avenue. Two people died at 8 Links Road, West Wickham, and a man and his 14-year-old daughter were killed at 29 Havelock Road, Bromley, the scene of this bombing now a block of flats.

Raiders flew over London on every night throughout October 1940. Each evening at dusk, or soon after, the wailing of many sirens announced the approach of the first wave of the night's unwelcome visitors. Typically, the bombers took a route via the Thames Estuary in crocodile line, then fanned out north and south; or they arrived from a SE direction over Kent. This approach posed more danger to Bromley, for it lay in the flight path.
Whatever their orders might be about bombing central London, the docks, or other specific target area, all manner of things could cause crews to release their deadly loads elsewhere - engine trouble, damage by AA fire, illumination by searchlights, faulty navigation, an encounter with an RAF night-fighter (rare at this period), or simply a reluctance to penetrate far into London's gunbelt. They had little to fear from the guns in the autumn of 1940, except fear itself. AA fire at night was inaccurate and the pilots usually flew above the ceiling of bursting shells. But it did have on many crews what the military called 'a moral effect'. It was supposed to have an opposite, i.e., good morale effect on the civilian population, ignoring those who were understandably unnerved by it.

The progress of each wave of bombers could be followed visually by the flash of guns drawing nearer, the star-like burst of shells, and searchlights probing fitfully among the clouds. Behind the crash of 3.7inch guns and other artillery pieces would be heard the sinister throb throb of desynchronised aircraft engines. The sound, so rapid in approach, seemed painfully slow in passing over.

"You never hear the one that hits you", was a frequent remark one heard; or, "If it's got your name on it, there's nothing you can do". If the first remark contained any truth, then the last thing many victims would have heard was the sound of the plane that sealed their fate. For example, the Reynolds family as they sheltered in Queen's Mead Road, Bromley. Thomas, his wife Henrietta, and their daughters aged 10 and 8, and their son aged 3; they all perished when the shelter was hit by a heavy bomb.

The Reynolds joined a growing list of families who lost two or more members in a single incident. On the 6th, three were killed at 6 Cherry Walk and two in Homesdale Road, Bromley; on the 7th, four died in Anerley Road and two in Worbeck Road, Penge; on the 8th., up to ten members of two or three families were believed killed in a direct hit on a public shelter in Anerley Road; on the 10th., three died at 7 Hillcrest Road, Bromley; and on the 11th, six died at 10-12 Anerley Park.

These incidents, and many more like them, clearly came not from concentrated bombing but from the random discharge of bombs by passing aircraft. They nonetheless gave a steady drip-drip of human death in one's neighbourhood; of gaps appearing in roads where houses had been blown apart by high explosive or gutted by incendiary bombs. Sooner or later at this rate one's own street, one's own home, was bound to 'catch a packet'. You and your family might go with the house. But it needn't be at home; it could be at work, out shopping, sitting in a cinema. Anywhere at anytime.

Although the GAF used radio beams which could locate targets on the darkest nights, there was in 1940 no real substitute for bright moonlight as an aid to navigation. Moonlight also had the advantage for the enemy that it was not amenable to interference by British 'beam benders', only by British weather. For several nights in mid-October 1940 a full moon suffused town and countryside in her reflected beams, and the Luftwaffe made the most of it.

On 15-16 October the heaviest raid on London since the last full moon led to four deaths in Willett Way and St George's Road, Petts Wood, including an ARP warden. Three more died at 25 Windermere Road, West Wickham.

At incidents in Hayes Lane, Hayes, John Foster, aged 8, died at no. 103; an elderly man, a boy and girl, and a Jewish refugee perished at no. 216; but two lives were also saved. Owen Parsloe and Walter Field of Bromley rescue service were awarded George Medals for bravery in rescuing alive David Stoner, aged 5, and his mother.

The *Bromley Mercury* (28 February 1941) reported that

"a bombed house in Hayes Lane had completely collapsed. The top floor with debris on top had fallen on occupants, leaving space of only two feet on the ground floor. Both men tunnelled under the debris for three hours. Mattress springs and bedsteads had to be hack-sawed and propped up in order to reach the victims."

Just as the first parachute mines had been used during the previous full moon, so again they were out in numbers on 17-18 October after an absence of two weeks. In the early hours Sydenham and Beckenham were shaken by the blasts of a pair coming down together. That in Bryden Grove, Sydenham killed several people and destroyed dozens of houses, the damage stretching as far as Kent House Road, Beckenham. The other exploded on the sportsground in Cator Road, Beckenham, injuring nine people and severely damaging large, detached Victorian villas. Shortly before, another pair had struck Lake Avenue, Bromley (three killed at No. 1) and Plaistow Cemetery/ Hilldrop Road, where it was UX and later defused.

The latter part of October 1940 also witnessed attacks on Farnborough Hospital (two direct hits; one person killed, seven injured); the destruction of Anerley Road Congregational Church; the deaths of Sidney Gammon, Headmaster of Beckenham County Boys School, his wife, and 18-year-old son at 9 Foxgrove Avenue, Beckenham (on the 23rd); direct hits on Orpington Station clearing sheds (two trains hit, four persons killed); and extensive damage to Shaftesbury Invalids Home, Coney Hall (two killed).

In daylight hours the *Luftwaffe* continued to plague SE England. There were five main attacks on Sunday, 20 October, involving hundreds of bombers and fighter escorts. At around lunchtime, an Me109 disintegrated over Plumstead at 25,000 feet in combat with several RAF fighters. The pilot fell to his death with an unopened parachute. The engine and much other wreckage crashed in Welling.

Lunchtime on Sundays seemed to be the *Luftwaffe's* favourite visiting hour. They were back again in force on 27 October at mid-day. It was then that an Me109 was shot down over West Wickham. The wounded pilot baled out and landed near New Addington Estate, where he was reputedly set upon by some angry housewives.

7) *Effects of a parachute mine at Den Road, Shortlands, 19 October 1940. As with so many large war-time bombing incidents, the wrecked buildings have since been so well re-built or re-developed that the passing observer is hard put to believe such a violent event could have once taken place.*

8) *Sketch of a defused one-ton parachute mine on a naval quayside in 1940*

CHAPTER 3

Back to the Stone Age -
Chislehurst Caves

Well, if you knows of a better 'ole, go to it.
(Charles Bairnsfather)

Judging from many accounts of the Blitz, it would appear that the overwhelming majority of Londoners spent their time during air raids shivering in Underground stations and garden shelters, passively awaiting their fate. In fact, according to a contemporary survey, at least 60% seldom took refuge. Very few acted from foolish bravado in this. Most simply had an essential job to do, and in doing it they played an active and positive part in fighting the war. Younger people were naturally loath to spend long evenings in a dreary shelter. They preferred to attend dance halls, cinemas, social clubs, and pubs, so far as conditions allowed; perhaps not taking proper cover until late at night.

Fatalists and those familiar with statistical probability preferred to take their chances in a warm bed on a winter's night. Wasn't it Winston Churchill, in his cavalier way with statistics, who said it took a ton of German bombs to kill three-quarters of a person? To be a successful member of the 'stay-in-bed' brigade required the blessèd gift of sleeping soundly through pandemonium, or the wearing of earplugs, supplied free of charge but unpopular because wearers could not hear what was going on!

It's doubtful whether more than a handful of Bromley residents took advantage of London tube stations. To have done so meant an uncertain journey each night in the black out to the centre of the target area. The caves at Chislehurst were far more accessible.

Of uncertain origin - though man-made, not natural - the caves are romantically associated with the ancient Druids and the Romans. Many of the chalk workings, however, date from the 18th and 19th centuries.

The caves were thrown open as a public shelter within a few days of the start of the London Blitz as a direct result of the public-spirited actions of the principal lessee, James Geary Gardner, and two associates. The 'Caves Committee', as they called themselves, were not popular with the Home Office or the Ministry of Health, which had condemned the caves as unfit for shelter use. Mr Gardner was almost certainly acting beyond the terms of his lease, which allowed him to grow mushrooms in the caves but said nothing of letting the general public take them over as an air raid shelter and makeshift home-from-home.

But who was going to stand up and quibble over narrow legalities when thousands of Londoners were being killed every week and public morale was at stake? Gardner's initiative was a godsend to homeless Londoners and all who faced the nightly wrath of an implacable foe without provision of proper bomb-proof shelters, while those of power and wealth watched their nightly ordeal from a safe distance.

The popular Press made no bones about whose side they were on. They gave their blessing to the venture and published maps showing readers how to reach the caves.

Conditions inside the cold and clammy chalk labyrinth during the early weeks of the Blitz were such as would have made Stone Age man feel quite at home. They are well-remembered by the author, who, having been unceremoniously blown out of his Catford home in September, was obliged, with members of his family, to live in the caves for some weeks. However, for a boy without an adult's responsibilities, the caves were also an exciting mix of magic grotto, unexplored black voids out of which strange beasts or ancient savages might suddenly emerge, and reassuring oases of flickering lights where families chatted quietly in a unique community with shared common hardships and common dangers.

People brought bedclothes, stretchers, even bedsteads for their comfort; hung carpets for privacy; and packed sandwiches and hot flasks for sustenance. Countless candles and oil lamps illuminated the murky depths with dancing lights. Hot tea came from a stand just inside the narrow entrance. For one penny a spoonful, cough medicine could be procured from a nurse who made regular tours. With water trickling down the rock faces and humidity verging on saturation point, anyone with a chest condition was likely to need frequent dosages. Nor were the caves to be recommended for those with, or wishing to avoid, rheumatism, arthritis, or tuberculosis. Yet, there were some who professed to find medicinal properties there.

Ordinarily, the temperature in the caves varies between about 50° and 60°F, summer and winter. Most people will begin to feel chilly when sitting fully-clothed for any length of time in a temperature below 68°F. The introduction of numerous stoves, candles, and human bodies produced a warm, moist body of air which rose to the cold rock walls and roof, causing condensation down the rock face, cold draughts around one's legs, and a kind of Scotch mist to hover above one's head.

Things became better organised and a variety of amenities were introduced in the fullness of time; the luxury of electric lighting, for example. This was after the present writer had left the caves, with mixed feelings, for evacuation to Somerset.

A woman reporting for *Mass Observation* spent a night in the caves in November. She said there was no space for her camp bed by 6pm. Regular occupants commandeered positions weeks before. Some took possession of alcoves, in which they installed tables, cooking stoves, beds and chairs, and which they curtained off. An Englishman's cave is his castle, seemingly. There was little privacy of that kind in the beginning; only dark shadows in the candlelight preserved one's modesty. Some families lived there day and night. Some husbands set out for work from there, and housewives took the 227 'scooter' bus to go shopping in Bromley.

The woman from *Mass Observation* attended a service in a newly installed chapel, sited where a natural dome rose above an improvised altar. They sang the hymn Rock of Ages. What else? No rocks are more aged in Chislehurst than the chalk of the caves - 80 million years or more. The Bishop of Rochester came to preach in this subterranean niche of the diocese. He, at least, had some legal right to be there, for the caves, or land above, were apparently owned by the Ecclesiastical Commissioners.

Family groups passed the evenings reading or playing cards. A gentle hum of voices rose from all corners. Turns were taken to queue at the canteen now installed. They stood patiently in line, holding jugs, teapots or cans for a share of hot beverage, cake and biscuits. Sanitary arrangements now included partitioned-off and disinfected toilets. Around 4am everyone seemed to wake up and cough for half an hour, then went back to sleep. At 5am electric lights came on and the canteen re-opened. Most people emerged from their damp blankets at about 6am, no doubt sharing the feelings of one lady who was heard to say, "I am not a snob, but what a dreadful place!"

Mr H.R.P Boorman, editor of the *Kent Messenger*, ventured to spend a night there. In his book *Hell's Corner*, 1940, he describes how trainload after trainload came every evening. To stand at the entrance as they filed inside was like being "at a cup-tie final, except that there were endless women and children pushing prams and carrying bundles of blankets, rugs, pillows and cushions". By the time of his visit proper bunks were installed, also ventilation, two canteens, a Red Cross centre, and even a 200 seat cinema. He concluded, "I am bound to say it was comfortable, though I am glad I do not have to be there night after night.."

The number using the caves in December 1940 was estimated variously at 6,000, 8,000 and 14,000. They included small groups of Belgian, Dutch and Polish refugees from the Nazi invaders.

In the space of three months, according to a report in the *Kentish Mercury*, ".... these misty caves, full of foul air and icy water trickling down rock faces had been transformed into well-lit, airy 'streets'". There were now three canteens serving 300 gallons of tea nightly; dartboards were fixed up everywhere; attendance at the cinema was by rota... a dance floor, gymnasium, and hospital facilities had also been added.

Laisser faire of the early days no longer prevailed. Marshals were appointed to keep discipline. House rules came into force requiring that there be no admittance or re-admittance after 9pm. No one under the age of 21 was allowed as an occupant, unless with a resident family. Pitches had to be kept clean and all rubbish removed. Stoves of all kinds were prohibited. There was to be no unauthorised sale of goods. No music might be made after 9pm, while complete silence was requested after 10.30pm. Making a market in pitches was forbidden, and if a pitch remained vacant for four days it became forfeit.

Exactly how safe were the cave dwellers? Only the largest bombs employed in the Blitz of the semi-armour piercing type were at all likely to have penetrated the covering of most of the system. A heavy bomb near the entrance would likely to have led to casualties and rock falls blocking the way out temporarily. Any UXB in the ground above would have certainly required complete evacuation, but a trial evacuation showed it took two hours to clear the caves of everyone.

In 1944-1945 the V2 rocket posed a bigger risk, due to its deep penetration and the size of the explosive charge. 2,000 people used the caves at night during the rocket bombardment. They might have been well advised to take themselves off somewhere else, for the Chislehurst area was a frequent target. Fortunately for them, no V2 fell closer than about 300-400 yards from the entrance.

Chislehurst Caves

Miles of Mysterious Caverns

9) Chislehurst caves interior.

10 The entrance to Chislehurst Caves as it was in the early-1980s. Thousands of shelterers from far and wide trudged through the narrow access night after night and out again in the mornings during the worst bombings of the Blitz. (Lewis Blake)

A bigger threat to the shelterers' welfare than anything the *Luftwaffe* might do probably came from crowded living among people of all physical and medical conditions, levels of personal hygiene and cleanliness, and perhaps some carrying easily transmitted infections and contagions. In fact, there appear to have been no serious outbreaks of transmittable illnesses. So maybe, after all, the cool, humid environment did possess some healthy properties?

CHAPTER 4

All Through the Night

How shall your houseless heads and unfed sides,
Your looped and window'd raggedness, defend you
From seasons such as these? (King Lear)

Wonder of wonders, the night raid on 1 November 1940 lasted only until 11.20pm, and the next alert did not occur until 6.33am, making this seven hour raid-free period the longest for London since August. As if to make amends for their lapse, German raiders were back three times during the following hours of daylight. Then, more wondrous still, on 3-4 November the capital enjoyed its first completely raid-free night since 5 September. Londoners habitually credited Germans with unlimited capacity for new weaponry and for springing nasty surprises, so they naturally thought the peaceful night portended some new devilry on their part.

They need not have worried too much; it was probably just bad weather over Europe that had kept the GAF grounded. However, once more the enemy made up for it. On the next night, London was subjected to the longest air raid of the war anywhere in Britain - from 6.15pm on the 4th until 8.20am the following day, a period of 14 hours, 5 minutes. During this protracted period single raiders came over at frequent intervals in order (they hoped) to create as much disruption to commercial and industrial activity as possible for minimal outlay of men and machines.

After the single night break, London was bombed for another 25 consecutive nights, with longer hours of darkness encouraging the enemy to prolong his operations. Even on the night of 14-15th, when the notorious Coventry raid occurred and henceforth the Blitz spread across the United Kingdom, He111 minelayers could not resist the chance to have a go at the capital in full moonlight.

Without wishing to detract in any way from the sufferings of Coventry, it is worth noting that 142 Londoners lost their lives and 430 were seriously injured on the same night that the centre of Coventry was razed to the ground. The Bromley area avoided the enemy's attentions, but Stanley Sargant, aged 32, who lived at 21 Havelock Road, was one of 15 AFS firemen killed (he died in St Alfege's Hospital) by a mine at Invicta Road School, Greenwich. The death certificate gives cause of death simply as "Due to War Operations". Havelock Road itself had been bombed for a second time at the beginning of the month, with a direct hit on houses which killed five persons at No. 60.

With much of the night spent fighting a large blaze in Walthamstow, the men of Springhill AFS fire station on the corner of Plaistow Lane and College Road were pretty much exhausted on their return. Before they could relax, however, vehicles and equipment had to be cleaned and tested, and everything scrubbed and polished.

These tasks were nearly done when the undulating chorus of sirens on the morning of 2 November sounded from Bromley police station, Page Heath Lane, Shortlands station, Grove Park, and elsewhere within audible distance of College Road. It was just after 10am and already this was the second alert since dawn. A low-flying raider aimed two bombs at the AFS premises. One fell by a bus stop, demolishing a detached house, but with no serious injuries reported. The other was a direct hit on the station. Station Officer, 'Jerry' Jerome, aged 32, was killed, also Fireman John Taylor, aged 27. Both were buried under debris, disturbed earth, and an overturned car. John Taylor had become a father two days earlier and saw his baby son only once. Mrs Taylor was not well enough while in confinement to be told of her loss.

Patrol Officer W. Hall told a local reporter, "I was in the yard when I heard the bomb falling. It made a terrific noise; just like an express train at full speed... the blast threw me into the passage. The air was full of glass. I was stunned for a few seconds.... One minute everything was peaceful and the next minute it was just chaos". The report went on to say that three converted cars and two trailer pumps were smashed and twisted. It described the station as housed in a large villa standing in its own grounds and was formerly a women's hostel.

Several other firemen were buried, including the section officer who was covered up to his neck but was dug out unhurt by a rescue party within minutes. Another was Fireman Frank Bax who informed the author over forty years later that he was buried in the bomb crater. He recalled nothing until he woke up on a settee in his sister's house in Freelands Road, with spinal injuries, concussion, and contusions to the head, the effects of which he suffered until his dying day. The site of the incident is now part of the large grassed roundabout where College Road, Plaistow Lane and Burnt Ash Lane join. There is nothing now to suggest to the whirligig of passing motorists that here long ago was another of the countless forgotten tragedies of Nazi bombing.

The raid of 9-10 November was typical for this month. It started soon after dark and lasted until morning, but with long pauses between episodes of bombing. 37 HE bombs fell in Beckenham, Bromley, and Orpington without serious effects, apart from two persons killed at 9 Sandford Road, Bromley.

What made the raid different for Bromley could be traced back to the poor opinion a certain Leutnant Max Probst, pilot of one of the raiding He111s, had of London's AA defences. He told his captors later how he regarded the AA gunfire as so ineffective that he habitually flew straight through it. There is nothing like over-confidence to bring a person down to earth, literally in this case.

Gunfire blew away most of a wing as Probst's plane passed over Chislehurst, the wing piece coming down in the garden of 45 Cranmore Road. From that moment the plane was doomed. Max Probst could no longer maintain control and he baled out into the grounds of Sundridge Park Hotel and was made prisoner. Moments later the Heinkel smashed into 26 Johnson Road, Bromley Common, demolishing two houses and causing the death of Mrs Alice Monday. She and six injured residents were trapped under house debris and plane wreckage; two aircrew were dead in the fuselage; the fourth crewman hung by parachute from the chimney stack of No. 14, having baled out too late for the 'chute to open fully. Badly injured, he died later.

All this made for a grim, not to say nightmarish, situation. Worse was to come. Mixed in with the plane's wreckage were thirty unexploded 50kg bombs, and the trapped victims could not be reached without disturbing them! The awful truth dawned on everyone at the scene that the whole street faced disaster. As minds worked on how best to tackle the situation, Sergeant David Grigg, a traffic patrol man of P Division, Metropolitan Police, arrived on the scene and volunteered to remove the missiles one by one to open ground across the A21 Hastings Road. One of the bombs was thought to be ticking ominously, but Sgt Grigg nonetheless gingerly carried them to a safe distance from the street's terraced dwellings.

During this tense and seemingly endless process, Dr Kenneth Tapper, head of Bromley's casualty services, a New Zealander, eased his way under the remaining bombs to give medical aid and comfort to those of the injured who were still trapped and understandably quite frightened.

Both Sgt Grigg and Dr Tapper were awarded the George Medal for their outstanding courage. Of Dr Tapper, who already held the OBE, the *London Gazette* wrote that on many occasions he had crawled under dangerous debris to give Blitz casualties medical aid. Several rescue workers were also officially recognised with awards for their courage and exemplary dedication to duty.

Though we may read much about the inaccuracy of RAF bombing raids on Germany in the early years of the war, by contrast we seem to know less about the GAF's own poor accuracy. Despite having a far easier task in locating and bombing British cities, especially London, German crews frequently expended much of their bombs in blasting fields and woods miles and miles from the intended target.

The following table provides the numbers of HE bombs and mines (in brackets) reported in local boroughs up to 2 December 1940. A large number fell relatively harmlessly in open areas, with many more falling in rural parts of Kent, Essex, Surrey, and Sussex.

Borough	Pre- Nov 1940		7-18 Nov.		18 Nov/2 Dec.
Beckenham	387	(+ 5)	65	(+4)	27
Bromley	357	(+ 7)	52		19
Chislehurst/Sidcup	391	(+ 9)	139	(+2)	51
Orpington	772	(+14)	176		13
Penge	103		8		1
Total	2,010	(+35)	440	(+6)	111
+ Oil Bombs	146		1		1

The first column includes Battle of Britain daylight raids, as well as night raids (hence high figure for Orpington). Of course, it was not much of a comfort to those who lost loved ones, or were injured themselves, or saw their homes wrecked, to know they were not the intended victims.

On the 4th, London's biggest fire was at St Mary Cray Gasworks, where two gasholders burned out, three lives were lost, and nine persons injured. No one seems to have been killed locally on the next night, a fact which added poignancy to the deaths in Reigate of two evacuated boys of St Dunstan's College, Catford. One of the boys was Robert Parry, aged 16 (a member of the Home Guard) whose home was at 26 Charterhouse Road, Orpington.

6-7 November witnessed light enemy activity in the early evening and in the small hours. During the first phase the Co-op store in Penge High Street sustained a direct hit which killed three and injured four and destroyed several shops. Probably at the same time one person died and eight were injured in Kingsdale Road, and another life was lost (died in Beckenham Hospital) when an HE struck 'Crantock', Bushey Way, Beckenham. On the following night Beckenham Hospital sustained extensive damage to roof and windows; Beckenham post office was severely damaged by blast; and one person died at 169 Venner Road.

On or around 10-12 November, Miss Mary Louisa Heppel, aged 94 and a former headmistress of Bromley High School, was fatally injured at 3 Palace Grove and died in Bromley Hospital where cause of death was given as "a) Shock, b) Senility. Air Raid Casualty". It was previously thought that Miss Heppel was killed in April 1941.

The night of 15-16th saw a heavy raid lasting several hours and involving over 300 bombers. The raiders expected to benefit from a full moon, but low cloud and rain of an Atlantic depression frustrated their hopes. As a consequence the bombing became widespread across the London Region.

So widespread that even Knockholt on the margin of the region attracted a pair of mines near Knockholt House and in Randalls Lane - three people were injured and houses and farm buildings damaged.

Beckenham continued to take punishment, with six killed, including a woman and her two sons, at 15-17 Kelsey Park Road. A pair of mines killed two at 108 Merlin Grove and injured eight, destroyed eight houses and damaged a further 225, and at 55-58 Greenways killed five (including a husband, wife, and their two sons, aged 9 and 18) and destroyed or damaged 77 houses. Caught between the two blasts, the pavilion in Elgood Field serving as AA gun battery HQ lost windows and roofing.

Mines on 16-17th included Walden Manor, Chislehurst, damaging houses, and a UX specimen in Oldstead Road, Downham. The latter was accidentally detonated by a RN disposal squad, spreading destruction right across Southend Village and Downham shopping area. Another at the junction of Beckenham Place Park (the road of that name) and Westgate Road damaged 50 houses. Its companion fell in Lawn Road at the same time (4.45am), destroying or damaging 100 houses.

Raymond Wattenbach, a Bromley schoolboy, recalled keeping an appointment with the dentist at 8 Copers Cope Road later that morning.

"His surgery was in a dreadful mess. The windows were blown in and the ceiling had come down, too... He told me a land mine exploded not far away. My dental appointment was postponed for several years!"

(The surgery was situated 800 yards from Westgate Road and 400 yards from Lawn Road)

November ended with HEs killing a mother and daughter and one other person at 35 Bromley Gardens, and a mother and two daughters at 186 Burnt Ash Lane. Meanwhile, Shortlands ARP managed to cause great disruption by reporting a spent flare with parachute attached on the pavement of Tootswood Road as a UX mine. Regional HQ complained about the continued confusion regarding objects dropped by parachute, expressing annoyance that 2,500 residents had been evacuated from their homes unnecessarily.

11) Springhill AFS Fire Station, Plaistow Lane in the wet autumn of 1939. A sneak daylight raider bombed the station in November 1940, killing the Station Officer and another fireman. (Lewis Blake)

12) On 9 November 1940, an He111 bomber shot down by AA fire crashed here in Johnson Road, Bromley Common, carrying a full bombload of thirty 50kg HEs. Mrs Alice Monday lost her life in the ruins of No. 26. All the crew except the pilot were also killed.

13) A moonlit night brought out enemy bombers the way a hot day brings out flies. On such a night, 15 November 1940, two mines fell in Beckenham, at Greenways and Merlin Grove, killing seven or eight people. The picture shows the effect of one blast at 103 Merlin Grove.

14) Two views of 3-inch gun site (Battery ZS10 in the London IAZ) on Hayes Common, Bromley (off Warren Road) in the summer of 1940. (Imperial War Museum)

CHAPTER 5

The Second Great Fire of London

"In the old days you'd gone anywhere to watch a good fire."
(A Londoner's comment after a heavy raid)

For the first few days of December 1940 the pattern of relatively light raids spread over the night continued. During one of these on the 4th, a one-ton HE wrecked a wardens' post in Queen Anne Avenue, Shortlands and led to the deaths of two wardens - Leslie Hurst, in his thirties, and Mrs Gladys Blinkhorn-Hay, aged 48, who lived at 'Glencoe', 6 Park Hill Road, Shortlands, which was then a private hotel. This made her next door neighbour of Lord Stamp of Shortlands, who as described later was killed with members of his family in 1941.

Subsequent raids in the month tended to be more concentrated, shorter, but less regular. The predictable routine during the autumn of an all-night raid every night was abandoned by the Luftwaffe. Henceforth, Bromley no longer knew what to expect from one night to the next. Breaks, albeit irregular, were very welcome, but the unpredictability made adaptation and the planning of one's personal arrangements more difficult, and perhaps made the raids harder to bear when they did occur.

On 8-9 December an estimated 400 bombers pounded London from early evening until 7am, producing the heaviest attack for two months. 1,700 fires were started and casualties totalled 250 killed and 630 seriously injured. It was effectively concentrated in central districts - Broadcasting House, Westminster Abbey, and the House of Commons were all damaged. The converse of such raids usually meant outer boroughs got off lightly. So it was for the Bromley area on this occasion.
A mine in Diameter Road, Petts Wood killed a police inspector at 98 Woodhurst Road, injured ten other people, and damaged 500 houses. Thirty HEs struck the diminutive borough of Penge, about half in the Crystal Palace grounds. Only one person was killed and three injured. And HEs in the early hours of the morning claimed two lives and injured four in Bark Hart Road, Orpington.

Not a great deal happened subsequently until the last week of December. Then a short, sharp raid in the early evening of the 23rd involved IBs in Penge. A family of four died at 30 Mells Crescent, Mottingham - Stanley Smith, his wife, Hilda, their son, Henry aged twelve, and daughter, Beryl aged two. The Luftwaffe was obliging enough to observe seasonal restraint over the Christmas period, with virtually no hostile activity against the British Isles for three days and nights. Perhaps the German aircrews felt they had earned a holiday break. The people of Greater London certainly felt they had.

Normal service was abruptly resumed on the 27th. An attack by about 90 bombers between 8pm and 11pm concentrated on Greenwich, Lewisham, and New Cross. "The warning went at 6.30pm and before long bombs were just raining down... Lewisham caught it bad. We pulled the settee out so we could lie down behind it. I tried to write but had to give up. Bombs dropped at Catford, Loampit Vale, Hilly Fields and all around. All Clear at 10.55pm. Peaceful after that." (Violet Tyler's diary) Up to a score of HEs also found their mark in the Bromley area, yet casualties were few and far between.

Although bombs and the casualties they caused were the worst part of any air raid, they did not constitute the whole trauma. In the Second World War an air attack on a well-defended target like London was one which engulfed people for miles around in prolonged periods of gunfire, droning bombers miles high, hefty, jolting thuds and vivid flashes of exploding bombs, albeit at a distance, skies lit up by crimson arcs of flame, and so many sights and sounds which defied positive explanation.

Then came the Great Fire Raid on the City of London, Sunday evening, 29 December. About a quarter of the entire City was destroyed in giant fire storms long before the German population learned about such horrors in Hamburg and Dresden. If casualties were small for destruction on this scale, it was no thanks to the raiders. The City had a very small resident population, and, this being Sunday; the Square Mile lay quite deserted by its teeming office workers.

The first wave of intruders - which were He111s of the GAF's élite path-finding or target-marking force - arrived over the target just before 6.30pm and delivered a steady deluge of incendiaries that started scores of fires in the City's crowded streets and alleyways. The follow-up waves had no problem after that in spreading the flames. They dropped 130 tons of 50kg, 250kg, and 1,000kg HEs, 'opening up' buildings so they burned the more readily, blocking roads to hinder movement and firefighting, and fracturing mains services, especially the water supply.

Over 20,000 IBs in about 600 containers swamped firemen's efforts to control the spreading conflagrations. Water supplies gave out at critical moments, and an exceptionally low tide rendered the Thames an inaccessible dribble in the mud. In addition to six conflagrations (designated area fires requiring 200-plus pumps each), there were 28 major fires (30-100 pumps each), 51 serious (11-30 pumps), 101 medium (2-10 pumps), and 1,286 small outbreaks (one pump affairs). Every available pump and fire appliance in the London Region was called upon to tackle this rampant disaster in the heart of the capital.

The LCC area mustered its entire resources of 1,200 AFS pumps and 140 LFB appliances, including 20 turntables and nine fireboats. 640 'first-line' pumps were also ordered in from outer boroughs, hence all the AFS units and professional brigades in Beckenham, Bromley, Chislehurst, Croydon, Orpington, and Penge were probably involved in the gigantic battle, while 300 pumps were ordered into outer boroughs from surrounding counties as emergency back-up.

No fewer than 278 firemen were killed or badly injured that night in the City's crucible of white-hot flame. Total casualties numbered 672 killed or seriously injured. Things could have become much worse had not bad weather conditions closed down airfields across Europe.

A considerable amount of blast and fire damage spilled over into SE London districts. To start with, several minelaying Helllls of Bomber Group 28 (KG 28) were among the raiders; these crews could still be relied upon to drop their missiles short of the designated target. Five or six mines floated down on Greenwich, Lewisham, and Beckenham alone.

Beckenham's pair of mines constituted the only serious incident in the Bromley area, as far as known. One collided with a barrage balloon in its descent and exploded in mid-air in the vicinity of Cator Road. A few moments later, at 6.47pm, the other exploded with great violence in Cator Road, near the junction with Lennard Road. It destroyed six large detached houses, damaged 420 houses, Holy Trinity Church, a couple of small factories, and wrecked Lennard Road ARP and FAP Posts.

Twenty people were injured. The only person to die, however, was 11-year-old Hazel Burgess, who perished in the shattered premises of St Christopher's Kindergarten School on the corner of Lennard Road. She lived at 24 Abbots Way but her father having died she had been spending the Christmas holiday with her aunt, Miss M Carleton, who was the Principal of the school. Post Warden George Nixon, the author's future father-in-law, carried the child's body out of the ruins to a waiting ambulance.... The death certificate gives the usual laconic "Due to War Operations" as cause of death.

The regional ARP officer visited the desolate site a few days afterwards. He referred to the great devastation to be seen and noted that furniture vans spent the whole day being loaded with salvaged effects of wrecked houses. "Morale of residents is very high and repairs to homes are proceeding satisfactorily", he commented. The Mayor of Beckenham was among guests at a party in March 1941 given by wardens of Post 5 in Lennard Road, who were described as a "devoted band". The adjoining FAP was damaged so badly that voluntary sums had to be raised for it to continue. The Mayor said, "Had it not been for the public spirited efforts of the wardens of Post 5, it is doubtful if the work would have been proceeded with at all."

The consequences of a heavy raid obviously did not end with the All Clear - not for firefighters, rescue teams, bomb disposal squads, site clearance workers, doctors and nurses, engineers of all the public utilities, to name only some; neither for ordinary office, factory, and shop workers, housewives, or others who simply had a job to do or a living to make. As for the injured and the bereaved, the greyness of the morning aftermath symbolised the months and years ahead. One hardly dares to think of the predicament of those trapped, probably injured with life ebbing away, under tons of rubble, water from burst pipes swilling around and leaking gas threatening to ignite or send them into a sleep from which they would never awake. Rescue might be at hand, but would it be in time?

On Monday, 30 December local commuters faced once more long and tiresome travel by train or bus to the City. Most lines were out of action for part of the day, so that many workers simply finished broken journeys on foot. The main rail termini serving south London suburbs had been wrecked and were still smouldering. Scenes of charred desolation greeted City clerks as they clambered over debris, negotiated muddy water eddying in the gutters, and skirted smoking buildings in danger of collapse.

They might find their places of work gutted by fire or reduced to a pile of fallen masonry. Most had lost count of how many times they had wearily journeyed in cold, crowded trains, delayed by blocked lines and UXBs, and frequent alarms, only to be confronted by the results of the enemy's latest handiwork.

They would never erase the memory of this particular day or the days that followed it: struggling with correspondence, book-keeping, dictation, typewriting... without heating, lighting, telephones, power for office machinery, functioning toilets, or hot food. Wintry air blew in through broken windows and shattered doors; plaster and thick dust covered everything in a white mantle; and the only water was that which reflected emergency candlelight in puddles on the floor. In the dark evening they had a repeat of the morning's journey to look forward to, made more trying by the black out. Then perhaps another disturbed night of bombs and gunfire.

15) St Christopher's School and Kindergarten stood on this corner of Lennard Road and Cator Road, Beckenham. These are the ruins due to a mine behind the premises during the great fire raid of 29 December 1940.

16) Searchlights in the blacked out skies of suburban London.

CHAPTER 6

Blow, blow, thou Winter wind

'Into my heart an air that kills
From yon far country blows.
(A. E. Housman)

One thing could be said in favour of the icy winter which held Britain in its grip in January 1941 - it discouraged unwelcome visitors from venturing across the Narrow Seas. Thanks partly to this, January and February were the quietest months of the London blitz. When attacks came, they were unpredictable in timing and duration and in every way that counted; daylight or night time, single raiders or waves of bombers, prolonged high-altitude bombing or low-level sneak hit-and-run intrusions - the population never knew quite what to expect.

On the night of 3-4 January, for example, Bromley area was under air raid alert between 9pm-10.30pm, 11.20pm-midnight, and from quarter past midnight till 3.56am. A very trying way to pass the night if one retired to bed at every All Clear. Next night it was 1.10am till 7.26am. On the 6th there were morning and afternoon alerts (twenty bombs fell on open ground in Beckenham and Orpington) and from 7pm till 11.20pm.

No sirens sounded at night on the 7th, but in the afternoon a string of single intruders kept an alert in operation from 12.54pm till 4.17pm. It was a bitterly cold day and the raiders made good use of low cloud cover. RAF Biggin Hill was targeted by one crew, the sick quarters being hit, and some 16 HEs fell on the surrounding area.

A severe evening raid, mainly on SE London, on the 11-12th by about 100 aircraft led to between 20 and 30 HEs and numerous IBs locally. The Luftwaffe got in more practice at bombing non-combatant woods and fields - Chislehurst woodland, Keston fields (near Blackness Lane), fields near Beadon Road, Bromley, also in Orpington, and so on. 37-39 Cator Road, Beckenham sustained some damage, and at the rear of Abbots Way a one-ton UXB on the railway embankment stopped all traffic on the mid-Kent line to Hayes. Elsewhere, however, people told local reporters that incendiaries rained down like a score of gigantic firework displays in one. One incendiary fell through a roof into a bedroom where a dead man lay in his coffin!

It was in this attack that the booking hall of Bank Underground Station received a direct hit at 6.30pm when it was crowded with homegoing City workers. The whole roadway outside the Bank of England and the Royal Exchange collapsed into the booking hall and pedestrian subways, creating one of the largest craters seen in London. 55 lives were lost here according to early reports and many more injured. It is almost inconceivable that among the casualties there would have been no one from the Bromley area, but the writer has no details of cases.

On the 19th some 40 bombers penetrated London's skies between 10.30pm and midnight. HEs were recorded in Julian Road, Chelsfield and Westerham Road, Biggin Hill at 11.20pm. But it was Elmers End which felt the worst of it. Some fourteen 50kg and 250kg HEs struck around the station. Emergency services reacted quickly. Beckenham ARP control centre received details at 10.39pm; first aid parties were on their way at 10.41pm, and a rescue squad was out one minute later.

In St Margaret's Road, alongside the station, a direct hit on cottages killed two persons and injured three at No. 10 and demolished or badly damaged the whole terrace. Later attacks put paid to St Margaret's Road for good. All the Victorian dwellings which backed onto the railway were swept away after the war, their place subsequently taken by business premises. A direct hit on the station destroyed a platform and uprooted 60 feet of track. One porter was cut by flying debris and suffered delayed shock. As soon as it was light, repair gangs began work and had the track ready again for use by noon.

Low cloud, rain, sleet and snow across Britain and the Continent prevented further bombing at night until the 29th, although it did not stop several forays by the enemy in daylight. In one of these at 3.40pm on the 28th, Manor Way and Stone Park Avenue, Beckenham were blasted by ten 50kg HEs, without causing any serious casualties as far as known. Wet and cloudy conditions accompanied enemy activity on the evening of the 29th. In Sidcup, Maidstone Park and Bexley Lane were bombed. A little earlier two half-ton bombs exploded at Farnborough. In Rowan Walk there were three fatalities at No. 41. The other bomb exploded in a pond at Farnborough Park.

Three raids in daylight on the last day of the month involved casualties and widespread damage in the centre of Bromley. At 11.15am a 500kg HE hit Tylney Road, injuring five persons. A second raider at 2pm dropped ten HEs and a container of IBs in the vicinity of the High Street. The blows fell just as stores were due to re-open after lunch break - most shops closed for lunch in those days. Several bombs expended themselves in the grounds of Bromley College, but another which fell at the rear of 14 North Street caused the death of Stanley Burton, aged 31, who lived at 78 Nichol Lane but happened to be visiting his father in North Street. A considerable amount of secondary damage to shops around Market Square and in the High Street meant many brooms were busy that afternoon sweeping broken glass and ceiling plaster into street gutters to be added eventually to the mountains of Blitz rubble accumulating in council depots.

Weather conditions were actually worse throughout February than during January, so scarcely any bombing of significance occurred anywhere in Britain. However, two persons were killed and 22 injured on the 5th in Blackfen Road, Sidcup, where a half-ton HE exploded in the front garden of a bungalow. Two more HEs of the same size caused no casualties.

Anyone in Bromley who may have been rashly thinking at the end of February that the worst of the Blitz was over was in for disillusionment. The first signs of spring brought out, not just the crocuses, but German bombers in greater numbers than ever before.

17) A direct hit on Carlton Parade, Orpington High Street on 9 March 1941 killed David and Celia Levy at No. 14. The site, cleared as shown, was later re-built to the original state. Now occupied by a Co-op Store and Unwins, wine merchants.

CHAPTER 7

The First of the Great Spring Raids

The stormy March has come at last,
With wind, and cloud, and changing skies;
I hear the rushing of the blast.
(W. C. Bryant)

In bright moonlight on 9 March the centre of Bromley came under attack soon after 9pm. There was the usual mix of HEs and IBs, the latter now containing, as often as not, an explosive charge with a D/A fuse which rendered them more lethal and difficult to extinguish than those in the autumn which even children were known to deal with. 250kg bombs wrecked the Express Dairy at 25a College Road and a garage in Hammelton Road, which housed motor hearses and other vehicles. The blast threw one hearse into neighbouring back gardens, while wheels and spare parts sailed over rooftops into bedrooms and living rooms. Only a large crater marked where the garage had stood.

On the other side of the town centre dozens of fires broke out. Mr W. T. Redgrave, a warden of Post C3 in Mason's Hill, was hoisted by colleagues through the loft trapdoor of a house in Sandford Road in order to tackle flames taking hold in the rafters. The timely arrival of an AFS trailer pump enabled the fire to be put out before the roof was burned off. The warden next devoted his efforts to dousing IBs in Pinewood Avenue by burying them in the soil.

A more important matter then demanded Mr Redgrave's assistance in Stanley Road where a fire was taking hold and starting to 'get away' at a warehouse filled with timber cases. Thick, choking smoke was already enveloping Mason's Hill, Bromley Hospital, and much of the High Street, as the warden went hurrying off to this new call.

S. Critchley-Auty, Bromley's town clerk, reporting on the raid, wrote:
"... one fire created a vivid glow in the sky over a wide area. Fireguards, organised into teams for the first time, pounced 'like tigers' on incendiary bombs. They put out all but ten fires before the AFS arrived. In one instance, fireguards were overcome by smoke and laid out on a lawn. Another was lost in black smoke in an upper room. A stretcher party leader with a wet towel round his face went in after him. He reached him with difficulty. From the smoke a voice asked for his torch, which by feel only he was able to place in his hand. That was all the help the other wanted, so the stretcher-bearer withdrew. After putting out the fire, the firewatcher emerged from the

building almost nonchalantly".

Half a dozen HEs and 150 IBs fell around Orpington High Street, with a direct hit on 14 Carlton Parade. David Levy and his wife, Celia, who ran a tailor's shop here, were killed and eight others injured. Ten shops in this parade were destroyed or severely damaged by fire and blast. Chislehurst was the target for some score of HEs, including nine in fields near Gosshill Road at 11.15pm. Three of these were half-ton UXBs.

The first of the four mass-attacks that brought the 1940-1941 London Blitz to a climactic conclusion occurred on 19-20 March. 500-plus bombers launched 450 tons of HE and 3,400 canisters of IBs (say, 100,000 incendiaries on a conservative estimate) over a six-hour period between 8pm and 2am. 630 Londoners were reported killed and more than double that number injured. 1,900 fires burned across the region, including several conflagrations, the bombing being particularly bad in east and SE London districts.

One wonders what pressing inducement on such a night caused a family of three to throw caution to the winds and wait for the last bus home by the post office in Mottingham. All around them the sky filled with bursting shells whenever the enemy came near. Jagged splinters from 5,000 heavy shells fired this night were a serious hazard in themselves. The flash and thud of exploding bombs at all points of the compass should have been enough to send even the most rash and imprudent under cover. The family would have strained their eyes in the black out in the hope of seeing the bus dimly heave into sight, but was there any real prospect of that happening while the bombardment continued?

The answer will never be known because a one-ton HE exploded in the roadway just thirty yards from where they stood. Razor-sharp bomb splinters cut them down in an instant. Dorothy Smith, wife of the sub-postmaster, and her son, John, aged eight were also killed, the boy dying next day in Queen Mary's Hospital, Sidcup. A sixth person died in the vicinity of the blast near the junction of Mottingham and Portland Roads. Among eighteen injured there were three trapped under burning debris ignited by a broken gas main. Rescuers tunnelled to them while the AFS played water on the fire, something normally avoided as it could to set off more explosions.

Other local incidents included the following:

Hillcrest Road, Bromley: four houses set alight by about 100 IBs.
Keston Park: one killed, two injured by 250kg HE.
Warren Avenue, Hayes: half-ton HE ten yards from Anderson shelter, three slightly hurt in shelter.
Kingswood Ave/ South Hill Road/ Ravensbourne Ave, Shortlands: dozens of houses set alight by incendiaries.

Mosslea and Selby Roads, Penge: several fires.

Anerley Road, Penge: ARP Controller fatally injured by HE.

Hockenden Farm, Chislehurst: several HEs (also on the Common)

Harcourt Road, Sidcup: D/H on No. 83. 5 killed, 3 seriously injured.

Warwick House, Sevenoaks Road, Pratts Bottom: 5 injured by mine.

Chelsfield Hill: UX mine broke up on impact.

Wheatsheaf Hill, Chelsfield: mine damaged farm buildings.

Tragedy fell upon the AFS of Coney Hall, West Wickham while fighting fires at Plaistow Road, West Ham. Five firemen were killed - C.W.M. Drew, D.G. Fitzgerald, F. W. Moore, L. J. Palmer, and S. Short. Five hundred people took part in the silent funeral procession from West Wickham fire station to St John's Parish Church, where the service was conducted by the Bishop of Croydon and the Rector, Revd. Lt. Col. C. A. Shaw Page, DSO, MC.

The raid on the next night, 20-21 March, was on a much lighter scale, involving about thirty aircraft. Lighter for London itself, that is, but not for

18) A 1914 picture of Brisley's Corner, Mottingham, the site of the incident of 19 March 1941 when this whole parade of shops was destroyed by a large bomb, including the postmaster's wife, their son and a family waiting for a bus. After temporary premises further down the High Road, a site was found for the post office and new parade of shops in Court Road, built on the field seen in the foreground. (Gus White/John Kennett Collection)

Bromley, due to the raiding force confining most of its attention to outer suburbs of SE London. Incendiaries were not much in evidence on this occasion. Instead, Bromley, Hayes and West Wickham had 87- 50kg and 250kg HE bombs to contend with, and Orpington another 15 - 50kg.

At three killed and 15 injured, casualties could be considered light in all the circumstances. Places affected included Bromley North Station (a hit on the goods sidings), Homesdale Road, Siward Road, The Chase, Park Road (near junction with Palace Road), Elmstead Lane, Turpington Lane, Hayes Common, and seven turnings in West Wickham, including Bourne Way, Queensway, Pickhurst Rise, Goodhart Way, Lime Tree Walk, Holland Way, and Westmoreland Road - 24 bombs in all, advancing like the shuddering footfalls of a striding giant.

20) Only the tower of Bromley Parish Church remained standing after a direct hit in the opening bombardment of the 'Bromley Blitz', 16 April 1941.

19) North water tower of the old Crystal Palace plunging to oblivion after demolition engineers set off a charge at its base, 16 April 1941. The barrage balloon seen in the upper picture on the right of the tower could be flying from Sydenham Wells Park.

CHAPTER 8

Ordeal by fire and explosion
And that inverted Bowl we call the sky,
Whereunder crawling coop't we live and die.
(Omar Khayyam)

After the batterings it received in late March London was virtually ignored by the *Luftwaffe* for nearly a month while it concentrated on its favourite cities and ports elsewhere in the kingdom: Bristol/Avonmouth, Glasgow/Clydebank, Merseyside, Coventry, Birmingham, Tyneside, and Belfast. The capital's turn came again on 16-17 and 19-20 April 1941, during which the largest assemblies of German bombers ever directed against a single target exacted a grievous toll on life and property. Following this, Plymouth was battered for a week, together with heavy raids on Sunderland, Merseyside, and Portsmouth.

One bright spot for the defenders - a significant one - was the increasing destruction of raiders by RAF night fighters, plus better results by radar-controlled AA guns. At least 40 He111s and Ju88s were confirmed shot down at night in April, with others accidentally crashing or failing to return to base without known reason. These losses were not yet prohibitive, but German crews were beginning to notice the change. An article in the *Völkisher Beobachter* (People's Observer) contrasted flights over Britain with those over other countries:

"In Poland and Norway and even in France last summer, it was a short mission and every mission was a holiday. Flights to England are quite different. Each time AA searchlights and night fighters have to be faced."

The Turin paper *La Stampa* (Italy was then Germany's ally) paid a glowing tribute to the RAF: "The ardour of British pilots is assuming gigantic proportions. The British people owe a great debt of gratitude to their air force. British anti-air defences and signalling systems are almost perfect. Not a single German plane can reach the British sky without being identified immediately after taking off."

The month's break gave time to clear away debris and shore up damaged buildings. Blessed peaceful nights. People had so recovered from a surfeit of explosions that hundreds lined Crystal Palace Parade on 16 April to witness another voluntarily - the blowing up of the north tower of the old Crystal Palace complex. After the great fire in 1936 the only significant structures left were two 284ft water towers. For reasons which the general public assumed were connected with denying German pilots navigational assistance, both towers were doomed in 1940. The south tower went first, dismantled from the top. Now demolition charges were detonated at the foot of the north tower, and Isambard Brunel's great creation plunged in a large cloud of dust to oblivion. Were the onlookers suitably impressed? Apparently not all; according to one account, some local veterans of loud bangs thought the smallness of the explosion a disappointment. If only explosions that very next night were as small!

Radio monitoring of air activity over France had indicated for some time that a heavy raid was being prepared. A record force of nearly 700 bombers, armed with 900 tons of HE and 150,000 IBs, were gathering for a night-long assault in which 1,200 civilians would die and 2,000 suffer serious injuries in the London area.

In Bromley, Civil Defence personnel (formerly ARP - a title which stuck in general use) stood ready for action when the alert sounded at about 9pm, London's 544th since the war began. It was none too soon. Reports of white route marker flares over Cobham and West Malling were coming in from wardens and Observer Corps posts. Chandeliers of red target flares over central Bromley minutes later were clear evidence that the town had been selected as an aiming point.

Bromley Parish Church was the first target to receive a direct hit. At 9.15pm a 250kg HE bomb left only the tower standing, and that was in no great shape. Blast sent heavy stones hurtling into the roadway, blocking it to all traffic, and seriously damaged properties facing the churchyard. Hazel Kissick, an 18-year-old pupil of Bromley County Girls School, was killed in the church while on firewatching duty - a grim reminder that teenagers aged 16 and over were required to serve in something positive for the war effort, despite the risks.

At 10pm, when tremendous cascades of IBs swamped the Market Square, the ruined church was among dozens of places to catch fire. An estimated 120 IBs showered Church House at the same time, starting a severe fire. Unfortunately, because Church Road was blocked by debris, AFS appliances could not reach the building. The blaze soon proved beyond the power of firewatchers to control. Next day only smouldering parts of the outer walls remained standing. The premises since August 1938 had housed No. 19 Centre, Observer Corps, (later Royal Observer Corps) which was responsible for passing on to RAF Fighter Command all observed aircraft movements over the southern approaches to London. The Corps were driven out in great haste as flames devoured the roof and swept down staircases to threaten their operations room. It was a case of jumping out of one fire into another. Bromley telephone exchange was designated the back-up emergency centre, but when they reached it through an obstacle course of burning buildings, falling bombs and AA shell splinters, they found it too was on fire and their help was needed to put out the flames before they could resume contact with posts in Kent and Surrey, and with the RAF.

At Dunn's furniture store in Market Square the first shower of IBs sparked off a number of small fires, which the store's firewatchers were able to extinguish, but then a larger helping of these hissing, fizzling, exploding missiles set light to the linoleum department. From there the flames spread quickly through all floors, driving the firewatchers before them. A number of AFS units were soon on the scene, running out their hoses.

It was a familiar story - the hoses ran dry due to fractured water mains and the blaze got completely out of control. The store was destroyed in an incandescent column of flame, which spread to adjoining shops. Edward Isard's gardening/hardware store was another victim of blast and fire in the Market Square - first wrecked by a 250kg HE and then set on fire by IBs. Other fires nearby at this early stage were Bromley Congregational Church (left a burnt out shell), *The Duke's Head* pub, the Homoepathic Hospital in Lowndes Road, the parish church vicarage, and Stockwell College (direct hit by 250kg HE set fire to the music room and other parts of the building).

By 10pm half the town seemed to be well alight, though the bombing had scarcely got into its stride. St Mark's Church in Westmoreland Road was burning furiously where a direct hit had caused the roof to collapse on top of rows of mangled pews. In Siward Road a large blaze involved houses, a garage, and a bakery. A laundry in Beckenham Lane, Shortlands was on fire, struck by IBs soon after a one-ton HE exploded on the pavement outside 43-45 Martin's Road, leading to the destruction of ten terraced cottages and damage to 270 houses, two laundries, and every shop in the village. Staff and AFS units were also grappling with a fire at Bromley Court Hotel.

Equally severe fires to those in the Market Square reduced to a charred skeleton the Methodist Central Hall and nearby properties in London Road, corner of Farwig Lane. With the burning down of the Central Hall, Bromley lost its principal venue for concerts, recitals, and meetings, never to be replaced. Only a month before the raid the famous Russian pianist, Benno Moiseiwitsch, was perhaps the last solo artist to give a performance there.

Joan Mortlock, living in East Street, wrote a few days after this raid and a heavy follow-up attack on 19-20 April 1941, as follows:

"It really has been like living through hell here this last week; plenty of people besides me have lost their nerve. I have never been so terrified in my life before and thought the house was sure to fall on us. I was up the road firewatching when the first bombs fell. There is not any of the church left, except for a piece of the tower, which will probably fall down at any moment. Dunns in the Market Square is completely gone, also Isard's warehouse behind the post office. I thought nothing of lying in the doorway in all the dirt as the bombs swished down.

"There was the continual cry for water coming from the darkness that was getting more and more into a nasty red light. It took me nearly ten minutes at one time to get a bucket of water through our shop as at every few inches I had to lay down owing to a bomb screaming down too close for my fancy. Mum, Ginge and I spent from 10pm till about 4am sitting under our basement stairs clinging to each other. It was freezing cold; the back door had blown in and the scullery window out; the back windows of the shop had also gone and the wind and blast of bombs just whistled through the place. "

Mrs Joan Ross, who lived close to the Market Square, recalled* that members of the Young People's Fellowship of the parish church had a rota for firewatching, and in pairs they spent the night in the vestry once a week. She was on her way out of the house to join Hazel Kissick when the air raid warning went and almost immediately there was a great deal of flak and the sound of German bombers overhead.

"My mother begged me not to go round to the church until things quietened down a little, and so I waited. There were incendiary bombs in our road, in our garden and those of nearby houses, so there was a great deal to be done, putting these out with stirrup pumps and buckets of water. The sad ending to this story is that the member of the Young People's Fellowship who was on duty with me in the church vestry was killed. I often thought that my mother's foresight saved my life."

How many like Raymond Wattenbach, at home in Plaistow Lane on Easter holiday from school, shivered in fear throughout this appalling night? Trying to sleep in the kitchen, he could hear the bombs exploding and the crash of glass in the centre of Bromley.

"It all seemed so close. It was the noise of the crashing glass and the drone of the bombers and the bombs exploding which made me shiver in fear. I suppose the echoes often resounded from exploding bombs, causing a kind of vibration."

It becomes clear that after flares had been used to mark Bromley, IBs were used by the bomber waves immediately following to illuminate the town so that later raiders, armed mostly with heavy HE bombs, would be able to locate where to concentrate their attacks with some accuracy. IBs were less in evidence in other south suburban districts, and it appears from reported

---

* *Both quotes taken from Memories of the Many...compiled by Paul Rason. (Environment Bromley, 1995)*

21) Church House, Bromley, circa 1932

22) Church House, Bromley, April 1941. The gutted ruins of Church House after a deluge of incendiaries set it ablaze, 16 April 1941. Almost the only recognisable feature from the earlier picture are the trees on the left of the building.

23) *Central Hall, Bromley. Another major fire on 16 April 1941 gutted The Central Hall, Bromley, seen here pictured before the First World War, with the Beech Tree pub in the background. The Hall was Bromley's main venue for concerts, exhibitions and public meetings. The remains were blasted again by a VI flying bomb in 1944, and it was never re-built.*

24) *4 Park Hill Road, Shortlands. The home of Lord Stamp of Shortlands sustained a direct hit and two near misses by heavy bombs in the raid of 16-17 April 1941. Lord and Lady Stamp, their eldest son, three housemaids, and the family's pet golden spaniel perished in the blast.*

times of HE incidents from Croydon to Erith, including Lewisham, that the bombardment of south east London was designed to start from the centre of Bromley and then to spread by natural 'creep', or according to specific orders, to the east, west, and north. On this view, Bromley was selected as the reference point from which the bomber squadrons allocated to SE London suburbs could develop their attack.

He111 minelayers joined the later waves to cause many of the worst incidents for casualties. In Bromley itself a pair of mines fell at 10.30pm in Bourne Vale and Ravensbourne Road. The latter fell a short distance from shops in the lower High Street. It was a direct hit, which demolished 19 Ravensbourne Road, a three-up-one-down Victorian house. Six people lost their lives to it, including the widow and daughter of Revd. E. Holroyde, one-time rector of St Paul's Cray. 54 shops in the High Street sustained extensive damage, along with 290 houses, Ayesbury Road School, and Bromley South station.

A second pair fell soon after midnight with disastrous results in Nichol Lane and Southover. 19 people were killed and 16 injured in the Nichol Lane blast. The mine exploded at the rear of No. 72, which was the home of the Randalls, a well-known professional golfing family. Percy Randall, aged 43, his brother William, aged 49, and their sister, Helen, aged 65 were among the fatalities. The Mummery family lost five members: husband, wife, two infant sons, and Mr Mummery's sister. With the destruction of 26 houses and severe damage to many more, devastation scarred Nichol Lane and Croft Road for many years afterwards.

600 yards away, the mine at Southover was another direct hit, this time on Nos. 58-62 of a block of council flats. It was equally grievous in its results - 15 residents killed and 42 injured. Fatalities included five members of the Sutch family, Ethel Childs and her two infant sons, and a married couple and their 12-year-old daughter. Nine flats and three houses were destroyed and nearly 500 damaged.

Among over 150 heavy HE bombs to strike Bromley not so far mentioned were the following cases:

- 85 London Road: Billiard rooms demolished.
- 3-5 Jackson Road: D/H on Anderson shelter. 4 persons killed inside. Bromley bus garage and 60 vehicles damaged.
- 41 Mason's Hill: D/H Morton Crouch, ironmongers (corner St Mark's Rd.)
- 64 Lansdowne Road: D/H on detached house. 9 persons killed, included 3 Lewisham detectives in house investigating a post office robbery.
- 66 Forde Avenue: D/H on semi-detached house. 3 members of Bowe family killed; husband, wife, and daughter, aged two.
- Hayes Common: At 9.34pm, 4 x 250kg HEs plus 2 x 50kg near HAA site and 'Woodside', battery HQ. One UX 250kg exploded at 4.15am.
- 154 Pickhurst Lane: D/H by 250kg UXB on bungalow. ARP warden killed

when bomb exploded 1pm, 18 April (41 hours after impact)

- Burnt Ash Lane: 2 x one ton HEs plus 3 x 50kg in Westminster School playing fields and on allotments behind Working Men's Club. All were UX and safely defused by BDS.

Mr D. Lewis, who lived in Simpson's Road, was spending an evening with Joyce, his girl friend, in Henekey's Bar, Bromley High Street when the back windows were blown in by the bombs in Church House Gardens and on the parish church. They left the pub in complete darkness and on passing Freeman, Hardy & Willis noticed IBs alight in the shop. Mr Lewis assisted a policeman to smash down the front door and put out two firebombs, while another at the back burned itself out. Covering the bombs with sand, they then left to continue home.

Having seen Joyce home, Mr Lewis went on to Simpson's Road. Just as he turned the corner there was an enormous loud bang and he was blown against a house wall. He found his home at No. 50 wrecked by the mine in Ravensbourne Road. His parents, however, were safe in a shelter. Hearing cries for help from Mrs Clark at No. 68, he investigated and saw she was trapped behind the kitchen door with her three children. One daughter, Doreen, aged 9, was cut to pieces in the face but still alive. There was no else around to help. The raid was still in progress with German bombers still to be heard. So carrying Doreen in his arms while Mrs Clark walked hand-in-hand with her son and other daughter, he and they finally made it to the warden's post at Mason's Hill, where a medical attendant took Doreen from him. Mr Lewis learned next morning that Doreen had died during the night. She was buried in Bromley Hill Cemetery near the chapel.

The war stopped for no man. Mr Lewis was called up into the RAF in June and the following month was allowed home from RAF Newtownards, County Down to attend the funeral of his grandfather, who had not been well since the mine explosion and had died from delayed shock.

There was no real abatement to the bombardment until after midnight. People say that they heard the All Clear at that time. One woman recalled that she had taken cover in the basement shelter of Harrison Gibson's department store (later Army & Navy) and gratefully heaved a sigh of relief when she heard the steady note of the signal. Scenes of some confusion met her when she stepped into the High Street. Among the flickering lights and shadows thrown up by burning buildings people slipped and tripped over winding hosepipes that clogged roadway and pavement. Broken glass and debris of all kinds crunched underfoot. Water ran in rivulets in and out of the tangle. Fire appliances from as far afield as Tonbridge and Westerham were parked in side streets. Others bumped over obstacles with bells jangling.

The air was heavy with smoke and the smell of burnt timber. Fragments of charred material floated down like dirty snowflakes unsure of where to go.

Shadowy figures clambered over various impedimenta, shouting orders and receiving disembodied replies from the glowing twilight. They lifted and carried and sweated and swore.

Then the sirens began to wail once more. Amid groans of "Not again!", the confusion increased. Voices called out - orders to take cover - the urge to get away while there was still the chance - to go on or to turn back - indecision everywhere. Wherever it was they went, the High Street emptied of those who had no duty to detain them.

It was reported to Whitehall that there occurred "a minor panic on Downham housing estate in which about one hundred distraught women and children invaded a rest centre reserved for the bombed out". That such a small affair should be reported to a government department showed how unusual events of this kind were, which reflected well on the composure and sang froid of the civilian population. Although the affair was never publicly mentioned, what amounted to a veiled denial appeared in the *Kentish Mercury* two days later. An ARP official paid tribute to the estate dwellers for the fine way they stood up to everything, adding, "There was neither panic nor riot." The gratuitous denial of a riot suggests that exaggerated rumours had been circulating locally.

The former borough of Beckenham reported 73 HE bombs and 5 mines between 10pm and 1.30am. There were also IBs, but on a smaller scale than in Bromley. At 10.50pm three heavy bombs exploded at the top of Park Hill Road, Shortlands; one in the rear garden of No. 2, a second on a garage between Nos. 2 and 4, and the third a direct hit on No. 4, 'Tantallon', the home of Lord Stamp of Shortlands.

Lord Stamp, Lady Stamp, their eldest son, the Hon. Wilfred Carlyle Stamp, three housemaids, and the family golden spaniel, had taken cover as usual in the basement shelter when the sirens sounded, but tragically none survived when the house was blown apart by the direct hit. According to accounts, another maid, Elsie Unwin, was found by her rescuers lying in a pool of water.

Lord Stamp's entry in the Dictionary of National Biography states that "by this direct hit the Germans did more harm to their chief enemy than they could have realised. In the difficult aftermath of the war, Stamp would have been an ideal negotiator between Britain and the United States which he knew so well."

Among many tributes was that by Sir William Wood in the *Sunday Times* of 20 April 1941: "Barely six weeks ago. Lord Stamp referred to the death of one of his colleagues, and described him as 'another victim on Hitler's murderous list'. Now in his prime, he himself has been struck down by the same hand. I do not remember ever seeing him agitated; even in the dark days before Dunkirk he preserved a calm which was an example to us all. As for the manner of his passing, I need simply add that he feared death no more than he feared life."

Lord and Lady Stamp, who gave many services to the Free Church movement, were laid to rest in Elmers End Cemetery (now Beckenham Crematorium); buried, as they wished, within the borough of which he was Charter Mayor.

Among the last bombs to hit the borough was one which exploded in the roadway at the junction of Wickham Road and Court Downs Road. A passing AFS tender and trailer pump a few yards away took the full force of the blast, which killed three firemen and engulfed the vehicle in flames. The injured and shocked driver, 29-year-old Carl Taylor, won the George Medal for his courage in going into the flames and by almost super-human effort dragging a seriously injured comrade clear and carrying him to safety. A group of Canadian soldiers nearby said it was the bravest thing they had ever seen. Three of these were believed killed as well. A former pupil of St John's School, Penge, Carl Taylor was known locally for his hairdressing business, 'Maison Carl', at 59 Beckenham Road.

A half-ton HE, together with two 250kg and one 50kg inflicted heavy casualties in Churchfields Road and Blandford Road, near Clock House station. At least eight lives were lost with the destruction of houses and shops around 76-78 Churchfields Road, and another three people perished at 92 Blandford Road. Mr Keen, who lived at 76 Churchfields Road, returned after firewatching duty to discover his home in ruins, with no hope for his wife and mother-in-law buried under the rubble; only his pet canary was brought out unharmed.

Next door, Mrs Brackley was luckier. She was upstairs with friends when the bombs dropped. She did not hear them coming. What she remembered was the house plunging into darkness without warning and herself falling a long, long way. Her next impression was of lying half buried in debris, staring at the open sky and seeing yellow flares burning brightly high above. She owed her life to a timber beam that protected her from being crushed. The others in the house were also saved, although one or two were slightly hurt.

In another house, Mrs White had given birth to a daughter that day. Both were rescued unhurt, and others escaped through a hole in the roof. However, her husband was killed in a neighbour's home while celebrating the birth of his child.

The fact that five mines in the borough appear to have claimed only one life must count as a small miracle. Damage from that in Border Crescent at 11pm comprised six houses demolished and 95 damaged; further damage occurred in the borough of Lewisham. There were six injuries.

Two mines at 1.30am were certainly a pair dropped by the same aircraft. That in the rear gardens of 11-13 Southend Road spread damage over a 600 yard radius and killed one person at No. 11. Damage overlapped with that caused by the second mine, coincidentally at 11-13 Park Road. If that was not enough, the destruction covered much the same ground as the pair of mines in Lawn Road and Beckenham Place Park on 17 November 1940. Another pair was in Kelsey Park (180 houses slightly damaged) and Pickhurst Lane, West Wickham, given as next to Barnhill School (130 houses damaged. No casualties reported at either scene).

Happily, not all parachutes carried mines. A Beckenham firewatcher seeing one descending ran indoors to warn everyone to "get out quick". Whether that was good advice is open to doubt. What actually came down were four burnt-out flare canisters; the parachute was described as beautifully made out of over forty yards of silk.

As in Bromley, a feature of Beckenham's experience was the high proportion of UXBs with D/A fuses (about 15 per cent of the total). In Beckenham, however, one UXB was a rare monster: a 4,000lb (1,800kg) 'Satan' - effectively the largest weapon in Germany's blitz armoury, except for the 2.5 ton (2,500kg) specimen which was scarcely used.

It would be difficult to exaggerate the extent of devastation and the number of casualties had the Satan gone off in a built-up locality. Beckenham was doubly fortunate in that it fell on farmland - 250 yards from Wickham Court farmhouse - as well being a UXB successfully defused by men with the most dangerous job of all in the Blitz - bomb and mine disposal. Bomb disposal was carried out mostly by Royal Engineers, also the Pioneer Corps, Royal Army Ordnance Corps, and Non-Combatant Corps (conscientious objectors). Mines were defused by RN officers from HMS Vernon, Portsmouth, but preparation of the sites, excavation, etc., was the responsibility of the army's BDS.

Penge, covering a much smaller area than other districts that later made up the London Borough of Bromley, was hit first by three 250kg HEs in Ridsdale Road and a large shower of IBs in Green Lane at 9.50pm. The HEs demolished Nos. 26-32 and 50-58, causing four fatalities at Nos. 48-50 and a number of injuries in St Hugh's Road. The incendiaries started a fierce blaze at the printing firm of Johnson, Riddle, which AFS units were unable to save from being completely gutted.

Among other incidents in the Beckenham-Penge area were the following:

- 242 Eden Way: D/H. House destroyed.
- Midland Bank Sportsground, Lennard Road: 250kg HE. A woman and her three sons, aged 11, 8, and 5 years killed while sheltering.
- Goodhart Way: HE on pavement. One person killed at No. 13.
- 53 Bushey Way: D/H. 250kg UXB. Exploded 5pm on 17th.

- 1-3 Cherry Tree Walk: 500kg HE. Both houses destroyed.
- 57 Foxgrove Road: 250kg destroyed house, 3 x 50kg in garden, also a 250kg near convent.
- Oakhill Road: 250kg destroyed the Congregational church hall.
- Crystal Palace grounds: 3 x 50kg HEs. Half-past midnight. Included UXB on the edge of the motor racing track.
- 14 Derwent Road and on corner of Haysleigh Gardens/ Croydon Road: 2 x 250kg HEs.
- Ridsdale Road: Hit again at 3.45am by half-ton bomb at rear of shops. Nos. 4-12 destroyed. Two other HEs came down with it in Anerley Park Road and Castledine Road.

In the district of Chislehurst and Sidcup the worst single event was at Queen Mary's Hospital. Three 250kg smashed down at 10pm; two fell in the grounds; the other fell directly on Ward 15, killing 18 elderly and infirm patients and injuring 36, most of whom had been moved to Queen Mary's from hospitals or nursing homes in London, either for greater safety or to relieve pressure on beds needed for blitz victims. Of the six London area hospitals damaged in the raid, Queen Mary's was the worst affected. It has been re-built on a new site since the war, of course.

Chislehurst was fortunate in having relatively few incidents, yet the heavy nature of the missiles more than made up for the numbers. Three pairs of silent harbingers of death fell gracefully by parachute on their unsuspecting victims in Beaconsfield and Harting Roads, Mottingham; at R. Klinger's works on the Sidcup by-pass; and in Cranmore Road and Elmstead Lane.

The first pair caused the deaths of eight residents and injured 73. The effects overlapped; 40 dwellings were severely damaged, plus 370 other properties to a lesser extent. Miss Hilda Barker recalled for *Memories of the Many* that in April 1941 they had got tired of using the shelter and on the 16th they were indoors when landmines dropped along Beaconsfield Road:

"At 10.30pm one fell at the backs of houses opposite causing deaths and much destruction. My mother and I escaped through the gap where our windows had been and were eventually found by a neighbour. He took us to his house and I received first aid treatment under the table, being badly cut about the face and head. An ambulance took me and other casualties to Queen Mary's Hospital, but this, too, had been damaged and I was returned to the first aid post at Mottingham. Later I was taken to Woolwich Memorial Hospital to be stitched up and was just coming round from the anaesthetic when the All Clear sounded."

In the case of Klinger's, one hit the factory itself, the other exploded in mid-air from an unknown cause. At any rate the parachute was found but with no sign of a crater. In Cranmore Road and Elmstead Lane the missiles fell in rear gardens. They claimed two lives and injured 42, damaged 534 houses,

25) A fierce blaze here in Bromley Market Square got completely out of control, 16-17 April 1941, leaving Dunn's furniture store and adjoining shops charred and tangled beyond salvage. Today the road off on the right leads into The Glades. (Kent Messenger)

26) Churchfields Road, Beckenham. The junction of Churchfields and Kimberley Roads, Beckenham. Ten lives were lost in this explosion, and several small shops and houses were destroyed.

Road, Beckenham. The same in 1980 shortly before the site was re-
residential use. It was one of the last bombsites in Bromley area to be re-
ewis Blake)

28) St. Joseph's Church, St Mary Cray, as re-built. St Joseph's RC Church was among many properties blasted by a mine explosion in St Mary Cray High Street, with heavy loss of life. (Lewis Blake)

and both made craters 60ft across and 20ft deep. One woman was killed with her pet cat at 8 Cranmore Road.

Mrs Kirk, who lived in Cranmore Road, remembered how she and her husband converted the dining room at the front of the house into a bedroom shelter for themselves and their three young children. They placed a large wardrobe packed with clothes in the front bay and installed a bed for their two-year-old daughter in the chimney recess. When the mine exploded, the wardrobe absorbed most of the glass but Mr Kirk, who was sitting fully dressed between the beds ready to go on warden duty at midnight, was knocked unconscious and badly cut by flying splinters. The first thing he knew of the affair was coming round and finding himself on the floor.

An internal wall toppled on the bed where the Kirk's two sons lay. Only thick feather mattresses into which they sank saved them from being crushed. They were smothered in dirt, plaster and brick dust when their parents got them out. After that the family scrambled out through the rear of the house and started to walk to the FAP in Willow Grove, until a passing car gave them a lift. Mr Kirk's wounds were stitched up at the FAP, but his family were taking glass out of his head, neck and back for years afterwards.

The older boy, aged seven, was taken to Farnborough Hospital because of blood all over him - to everyone's relief it turned out to have dripped from his father's wounds when he rescued him. The younger son, aged five, developed a nervous stutter a week or so afterwards which went on for years and years - a not uncommon delayed reaction to severe shock.

A one-ton bomb at the rear of 52-54 Westdean Avenue, Blackfen demolished six houses and caused two deaths. Another one-tonner or 'Hermann' blew up behind 33-39 Beverley Avenue, Mottingham. Strictly speaking, it could have been an 'Esau'. The Hermann sobriquet applied to 1,000kg bombs of the thin-walled blast type. The 1,000kg thick-walled, penetrating bomb was dubbed Esau - son of Isaac and Rebecca, who became a hunter and ancestor of the Edomites who were enemies of the Hebrews. The distinction between the two bomb types is not usually found in ARP records. Sometimes an educated guess is possible from the nature of the damage reported.

Being partly rural in those days - embracing, for example, Cudham, Chelsfield, Downe, Biggin Hill, Knockholt, etc. – the district of Orpington could absorb a large amount of enemy attention without the scale of casualties and damage which a more densely populated place would expect. This did not alter the statistical chance of becoming a casualty if you heard the whoosh or whistle of falling bombs. It was just that if you were a casualty, you might well be the only one. Not a great comfort for you, but better for the community at large!

So it came about on 16-17 April 1941 that among the 47 HEs, 3 mines, and numerous IBs recorded in Orpington, only one incident caused serious casualties.

This was a parachute mine, which smashed into St Mary Cray High Street at 9.55pm. Eleven people lost their lives at Nos. 127, 162, 168, 172, and 176. The injured numbered 42. Among those who died was Mrs Rebecca Moore, aged 70, who ran the marine store at No. 176. She succumbed to her injuries next day in Orpington War Memorial Hospital. The point of impact was opposite the Catholic Church. Six shops and 31 cottages were destroyed, and 340 other properties, including the Catholic Church, were damaged. Several vehicles burst into flames, their petrol tanks blowing up before AFS pumps could really get to the scene. So much destruction tore the heart out of the old village.

Mrs Noreen Gillespie related for *Memories of the Many*, that she lived in East Drive, St Mary Cray and 16 April 1941 was the eve of her birthday.

"That night the sounds of bombs exploding were very loud and we realised they must be close by. We prayed our Dad would be safe. Dad was a constable in the Police War Reserve based at St Mary Cray Police Station, and he was on night duty. Eventually morning came, then he arrived looking so tired and sad. His first words were, 'Happy birthday, Noreen, thank God I've lived to see it'. Then he turned to my mother and said, 'Our church, our school, our presbytery, they have all gone. People have been killed and houses and shops in the village have been destroyed. I will never forget my ninth birthday! Dad lived to the age of 80 and my mother to 91. We were fortunate indeed - so many people were not."

The other mines came down at Biggin Hill, on fields and woods 500 yards west of Norheads Lane and 40 yards south of Crown Ash Hill. No casualties or damage to property was reported. The mines might have given the airfield a bit of a shake at two o'clock in the morning, but they were not the only 'bumps in the night' to keep the RAF station awake. Every so often heavy thuds of big explosions carried across open countryside from the directions of Cudham, Badgers Mount, Keston, Chelsfield, close by in Jail Lane, even Halstead, Shoreham, and Brasted. To those who stayed awake - and who could sleep? - it sounded as if every village in Kent was being picked on. Then there were those crimson glows over Croydon, Bromley and Orpington, which were hardly conducive to dreamless slumber if one dwelt upon the implications.

Incendiaries set light to a considerable number of houses in Newstead Avenue, Crofton Road, Pound Hill, and other Orpington turnings. The roof of Farnborough Parish Church broke out in flames soon after the raid started. Fortunately, firewatchers and the AFS were able to contain the fire before it took hold. Sunnyside in Tubbenden Lane was not so lucky. Hit by the contents of three or four IB canisters - about 120 firebombs - the house, which was once the home of George Allen, publisher of John Ruskin's works, quickly went up in flames and was reduced to a blackened shell.

The last of the raiders departed in good time to clear the country before dawn broke, so that at 4.30am the welcome sound of the All Clear filled the smoky air. However, life was not ready to return to what passed for normality in 1941. Smoke still hung over smouldering buildings in scores of places. At Siward Road, for instance, this lasted for three days and nights. Rescue work continued at several sites, including the flats at Southover.

Lord Stamp's second son hurried over from Epsom, where he was director of an Emergency Public Health Laboratory, as soon as he received news of the bombing. He arrived at his parents' ruined house in Shortlands just as the All Clear sounded. All day he waited and watched as his parents' bodies and those of his brother and other victims were dug out by toiling rescue workers. No one ought to speculate on what mental agonies accompanied a vigil of this sort, repeated all too often after every raid. Yet we may be sure he silently prayed the outcome would not be as bad as it seemed, whilst knowing it was too late for prayer.

The law assumed that the elder son survived his father by a split second and therefore legally inherited the title as second baron. Consequently, the younger brother's title was third baron. Lord Stamp was the only Peer of the

Realm to be killed by enemy air action in Britain during the Second World War; in the Guinness Book, his eldest son appears as holding a peerage for the shortest time in recorded history.

In Bromley alone some 1,500 people were rendered homeless. More than 4,000 homes were destroyed or substantially damaged. It took a month to carry out emergency, or 'first aid', repairs on those which were not write-offs. Nearly all train services were suspended south of the Thames for some days. A steady stream of relatives called at Bromley mortuary to trace or identify missing persons. Bromley's town clerk, S. Critchley Auty, reported how disturbed he was that people had to go through this ordeal but he could think of no alternative.

For ten days hundreds of people relied on emergency feeding provided by the council because of the failure of domestic power supplies. 34 roads in the town were blocked or closed by craters, debris, or UXBs. There had been 349 fires in the former Bromley borough - apart from numerous minor cases involving fences, sheds, greenhouses, and the like. 108 were large enough to need the attention of the AFS and local brigades, while 241 property fires were extinguished by the prompt actions of wardens, firewatchers, and householders desperate to save their homes.

Occasional explosions continued to rock neighbourhoods for hours afterwards with the detonation of UXBs whose D/A fuses activated before bomb disposal squads could deal with them. Some 40 UXBs were defused by BDS in the Bromley area, but at least another eight exploded without warning. A total of 300 HE bombs, over half in the old municipal borough of Bromley, 18 parachute mines, and many thousands of IBs hit the area. Many towns have been laid waste by less. Yet Bromley was not obliterated. For this it could thank in large degree its many open spaces, large gardens, and relatively low density of housing.

Exact figures for casualties are difficult to ascertain, bearing in mind that some victims died of injuries days, weeks, or months later, in some cases outside the borders of the Bromley area and therefore not traceable through local records. There is also believed to be an element of under-counting in the official lists overall. A figure for fatalities of between 140-150 in the five former boroughs and districts of this account is regarded by the writer as reliable, with the seriously injured (hospitalised) at around 160-180. The figure for the slightly injured who sought treatment at FAPs lies between 250 and 300. Many more simply treated themselves at home or possibly visited a GP in due course.

Picture Post devoted a special article by Louis MacNeice to the raid in its issue of 3 May 1941:

"They made a night of it: many people, both British and German, have called it the Biggest Raid Ever. It certainly sounded so - like all the banging of all the tea-trays and the loosing of all the fireworks and the rumbling of all the tumbrils and the breaking of all the oceans of the world. Just one long drawn-out lunatic symphony". Wandering round London, I thought the damage overwhelming. Hospitals and clubs and churches and luxury restaurants, tiny shops and department stores, flats and tenements and homes of all kinds, were shattered or scattered, spread-eagled or gutted. " The whole place", I said to myself, "has fallen to bits overnight!"

"Thursday, April 17, 1941 was a day with a very strange feeling in the air - partly hysterical, partly fatalistic, but partly - I should like to say - epic."*

Mr Critchley Auty reported the matter with less adornment:

"The spirit of the public was magnificent: courage, thoughtfulness for others. gratitude for services rendered, and a cold, unshakeable resolve to smash the terror by night and obtain just retribution is universal."

Germany began to learn the meaning of these words one year later, when the potential of RAF Bomber Command's new-found might and effectiveness first showed itself over Lübeck, Rostock, and Cologne.

---

* *Reproduced by permission of Mirror Pix.*

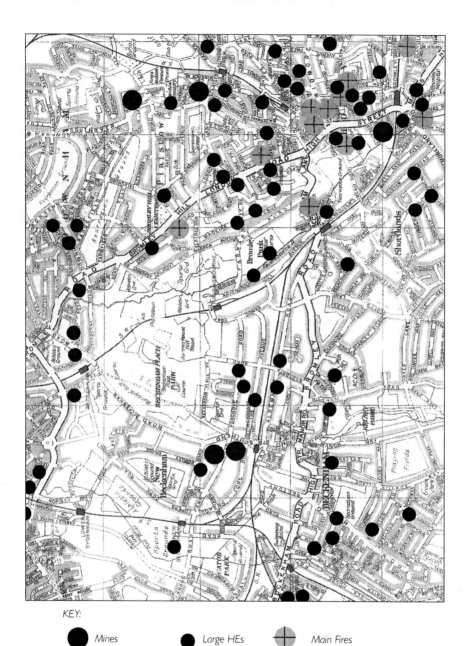

KEY:

⬤ Mines   ⬤ Large HEs   ✛ Main Fires

29) *Map of incidents, 16-17 April 1941. Approximate distribution of principal incidents in central Bromley and Beckenham and on border with Lewisham, 16-17 April 1941. (Lewis Blake)*

CHAPTER 9

Climax after the Blitz

'... it was the season of Darkness, it was the spring of hope...
(Little Dorrit - Charles Dickens)

Three nights after the Bromley Blitz and long before the effects had worn off, the GAF delivered the third of its heaviest spring raids on the London area. The most grievous blow for the Bromley area occurred miles away in London's East End. It happened on 19 April at Old Palace School, St Leonard's Street, Bromley-By-Bow. Men of Beckenham AFS were sent with four appliances to the AFS sub-station in the school and were mustering before going out to assist their East End comrades when a direct hit demolished much of the building and set it ablaze. Only an hour earlier these men were on stand-by at Woodside fire station to help Croydon contend with a spate of fires, if called upon. Now the entire contingent - 21 men - were dead, along with 13 firemen from elsewhere.

This disaster brought the number of Beckenham AFS men killed in the Blitz to 29, giving it what is believed to be the highest loss rate among AFS organisations in the country. At St George's Church a funeral service was held for 19 of the victims, followed by the biggest funeral procession ever witnessed in the borough. Some 500 firefighters from all parts of London and beyond marched solemnly behind a flower-bedecked fire engine and a line of motor hearses to Elmers End cemetery for a mass burial. (The other two victims were interred at West Wickham). Revd. F. W. Boyd, Rector of St George's, declared that "Beckenham will never, never forget those 21 fine young fellows who have given their lives for us."

However, Beckenham did forget. For about six decades, the nation as a whole also forgot the great sacrifices made by the wartime fire services. Only recently have successful efforts been made to remember and honour them with their own memorial and annual service in London. The men of Beckenham AFS who died in the war have now been honoured by commemorative services at Beckenham Crematorium in recent years, attended by civic figures.

Saturday, 19 April 1941: Alert lasted from 9.20pm until 4.46am. A rainy night with low cloud obscured the target area. Some 712 bombers took part, according to German claims, making it larger even than the previous Wednesday raid. It was the first and only time the enemy claimed to have dropped over 1,000 tons of HE in a single raid. Included in that were four

2,500kg 'Max' blockbusters and some 250 mines. 150,000 IBs were also unloaded on the capital. The death tally was put at 1,200, plus 1,000 seriously injured. The fire services tackled 612 fires in the LCC area and 848 in Outer London boroughs.

Two mines descended on Sundridge Park Golf Course and in Elmstead Wood, adjoining the links. Sundridge Park Hotel sustained some damage. Another pair came down in Parish Wood, Sidcup, north west of Berwick Crescent and west of Raeburn Avenue. A large number of houses were slightly damaged and two injuries were reported. Yet a third pair again fell fairly harmlessly on open ground - this time in Downe, 250 yards west of the High Street, opposite North End Lane, and in fields rear of The Rookery.

Aside from these six mines, the Bromley area was attacked with 101 HE bombs, the great majority now 250kg or heavier. The most serious instances concerned a direct hit on the trench shelter at Martin's Hill Recreation Ground (five killed); four HEs at Elmers End, where once again St Margaret's Road and St Margaret's Villas in Croydon Road by the station were blasted (eight killed in the villas, plus three killed by a direct hit on an Anderson shelter, rear of the station yard); at the station a siding and railway trucks were destroyed, and Muirhead's factory was damaged by a UXB. In other incidents, Bromley gasworks suffered blast damage, while in Crown Lane a half-ton bomb destroyed four houses and caused injuries to eight people.

At 39-41 Harland Avenue, Sidcup a half-ton HE claimed five lives (three adults and two children) and injured eight. In Elmington Road two persons were killed by a 250kg HE. Several HEs burst on Ravensworth Road School grounds in Mottingham. Keston church was badly damaged by a bomb in the churchyard, and in Orpington, around Poverest Road - Forest Way, a number of HEs fell causing one death.

10-11 May 1941: The culmination of the London Blitz, this was the most destructive raid for central districts of the capital. There were actually fewer raiders this time - a two-phase bombardment, with 358 bombers in the first phase and 148 in the second - but they managed a high level of concentration. Much less bombing over spilled on semi-rural parts of outer London than on many previous occasions. A major factor in this success for the *Luftwaffe* was clear, moonlit conditions across southern England.

Casualties were at an all-time high for anywhere in the UK on a single night: 1,436 people killed and 1,800 seriously injured. Up to this time nothing approaching such wholesale slaughter had been meted out by RAF Bomber Command. Yet for months Germany had been sowing the wind with gratuitous and indiscriminate assaults on Britain's civilian populations, never deigning to think that one day it might reap the whirlwind.

The alert lasted from 11pm until 5.50am. 1,863 fires burned in the LCC area, including two conflagrations, eight major fires, and 43 serious fires. For the first time ever, military assistance was called for at 4am to help London's swamped fire services.

The principal incidents in the Bromley area were as follows:
West Wickham: 4 x 250kg and 2 x 50kg HEs in Pickhurst Rise at 11.55pm. Five people killed at Nos. 108-112. Several houses destroyed.
West Wickham station: Direct hit on platform.
Beckenham: About a dozen HEs in South Eden Park Avenue, Beckenham Road, Sheringham and Witham roads (near Birkbeck station), and Kendal and Sidney roads (near Clock House station)
Elmers End: 3 x one ton HEs in Croydon Road at 3.15am. Smith's Instruments factory set on fire. Blast damage to the Elim Chapel and the Royal Oak Laundry.
Elmers End station: Bombed for the third time in 1941. D/H on Addiscombe branch line; parked train damaged.
Bromley: Widmore Road. D/H on No. 134. One killed, four injured; Wharton Road, one killed, three injured; Palace Road and Park Grove - six injured; several other HEs in Freelands and Park Farm Roads.
Sidcup: Crombie Road. 250kg HE. 0.35am. Child killed, four persons injured, three houses destroyed; Valliers Wood Road, Halfway Street, Forest Way - nine injured.

To all intents and purposes the London Blitz ended on 10-11 May 1941. The general public had no way of knowing this was the case; from their worm's eye view the evidence pointed to a continuation of heavier and heavier attacks for the indefinite future, until London was just one huge bomb-site. They were not to know that the bulk of the German bomber force was about to be shifted to support the imminent invasion of Soviet Russia. Eventually the *Luftwaffe* became as bogged down on the Eastern Front as the German army itself, so it was never again available in sufficient force to resume the wholesale pulverisation of London.

During April and the first half of May, some 70 He111s and 45 Ju88s were shot down at night, or were lost over Britain and coastal waters due to other causes. Of these about twelve He111s and five Ju88s were engaged in raids on London. The lion's share of all 'kills' went to RAF night fighters; AA guns accounted for about ten directly, but almost certainly crippled others; barrage balloon cables brought down two; and searchlights illuminated targets or assisted night fighters by 'pointing to' raiders' positions.

June 1941: The month passed with only a couple of incidents of any note locally. Just after midnight on the 5th a single aircraft unloaded on Farnborough Village one 250kg HE, 30 IBs and an oil bomb. The HE fell behind the Vicarage in Farnborough Hill, severely damaging the property, and ten yards from 'Hillcrest', which was partly demolished. The IBs fell without much effect around the intersection of the High Street and Church Road. A more

30) The largest funeral procession in Beckenham's history assembles in Church Hill, April 1941. Twenty-one young Beckenham AFS firemen were killed in London's East End in the raid of 19-20 April 1941. 500 of their comrades from all over the London area marched in solemn silence to Elmers End Cemetery in spring sunshine for the mass burial of nineteen of the victims.

curious result came from the OB, which exploded by a footpath thirty yards east of Church Road but failed to ignite.

A test by Orpington ARP next day of unburnt oil spread over a wide area of grass revealed traces of mustard gas. Further investigation was hindered by children having already removed most pieces of the bomb and by cattle having wandered over the scene, but a police guard was set up. Orpington's decontamination squad arrived to treat the affected area with bleach powder, while further tests showed free chlorine on contact with dry bleach and noticeable discolouration of gas detector paper. So as not to create alarm, the police advised onlookers that what they were seeing was purely a training exercise. Laboratory tests confirmed a mustard gas content of less than one per cent, for which no reliable explanation could be given. The conclusion reached was that the gas was due to some accidental exposure or contact in the manufacture.

31) Elmers End Station looking the worse for wear in the spring of 1941, having been bombed on three separate occasions. Track and platforms were destroyed, 19 January 1941; trucks and a siding were destroyed 19 April 1941; and a parked train was blasted by a direct hit, 10 May 1941.

At 1.45am on 22 June a passing He111 released a pair of mines on Crouch Farm, Crockenhill. One came down in an orchard, the other 150 yards north-west of the farm, off Crockenhill Road, causing damage to greenhouses. These were the last parachute mine incidents of the war in the south eastern part of London Civil Defence Region, and possibly the last, or among the last, anywhere in Britain intentionally aimed at civilians.

Despite lack of serious raiding by the much-depleted bomber force in France, air raid alarms of short duration were not uncommon in Bromley in the summer of 1941; not infrequently they came accompanied by spasms of AA gunfire. What usually triggered them was a token raider or two sent over for a mixture of motives. Probably important among them was the aim to tie down as many RAF and British army units as possible in home defence, for the minimal use of German men and machines.

28 July 1941: This was an exception to the above statement. The *Luftwaffe* mustered what must be considered a maximum effort against Britain for this period - just 60 bombers. They attacked east and SE London in what turned out a sharp, swift and very noisy affair, much more like a fierce battle than the leisurely one-sided bombardments of previous experience.

32) *Wardens Post C3, Mason's Hill, Bromley, circa. March 1940. From here Mr W. T. Redgrave and his colleagues carried out the onerous tasks of the warden service in the immediate neighbourhood throughout the war years. (W. T. Redgrave)*

In Beckenham a direct hit on 13 Thesiger Road at 2.15am killed four members of the Batstone family, including a 10-month-old baby. A second bomb destroyed a pair of semis in Knighton Park Road, causing the death of one person. Minutes later, Layhams Farm at Keston was struck by HEs of 250kg, 500kg, and 1,000kg weight. These hefty explosions not far away left Mrs Kennedy in Addington Village seemingly unmoved. "First night raid for weeks", she noted laconically in her diary.

Ruxley Farm over at Sidcup was another recipient of a plane's full bomb load, viz., three 250kg and one 500kg. Like Layhams Farm, there were no reports of damage or casualties.

In total Beckenham recorded 32 HEs; Bromley recorded 15; and Chislehurst/ Sidcup the four mentioned at Ruxley Farm. Given the size of the missiles and the typical bomb capacity of Ju88s at the time, these figures suggest eight or ten raiders (say, 15% of the force that set out from base) bombed the Bromley area in a welter of heavy gunfire. Two Ju88s in this raid were shot down by RAF night fighters. One blew up in mid-air near Horsham, scattering pieces of aircraft and crewmen across fields and cottages. The other exploded in mid-air with equal violence, over the Thames Estuary off Sheerness.

No further enemy visitations of any consequence occurred in Bromley until January 1943, the longest break from air attack of one form or another in the whole war. During this peaceful lull London's defences steadily improved until they offered a formidable obstacle to hostile aircraft. A prominent role in this process was played by the Home Guard, who had long since discarded the improvised and temporary amateurism of the Dunkirk period. They now manned AA batteries at weekends and at nights, so relieving Royal Artillery personnel for overseas duties. For ground fighting, pitchforks and broomsticks had given way to Browning, Lewis, Hotchkiss, and Vickers automatic weapons; Sten guns, Thompson sub-machine guns, and all kinds of bombs and mortars, such as the Spigot mortar which could fire a 14lb bomb half a mile. And the homemade 'Molotov cocktail' - a danger to all concerned - was discarded, along with other improvisations of the 1940 invasion summer.

A soldier's rifle is his best friend and that went for the Home Guard, too. Rifle drill at the local TA barracks or drill hall, stripping and re-assembling, cleaning, and 'the naming of parts' were essential in the training of what was basically an infantry force. Firing practice of the .303 was held at Hawkwood Lane, Chislehurst, among other places. Heavier weapons like the Northover grenade projector were tried out on Sundridge Park Golf Course. With an HAA battery in the park as well, one had more than golf balls to watch out for!

Field exercises were treated very seriously, the 'enemy' being not infrequently famous infantry regiments. A typical exercise started at 4am, Sunday, 27 July 1941. The 19th County of London (South Suburban Gas Company) Battalion was detailed to defend Sydenham Gasworks against companies of the Grenadier Guards, the Rifle Brigade, the Royal West Kent Regiment, and the West Nova Scotia Regiment. The fighting and skirmishing went on all day with, one hopes, the Home Guard left in possession. A loud and hectic air raid that night (described above) must have ruined the well-earned sleep of the participants.

The long lull in raids was most welcome among Civil Defence units. In the spring of 1940 morale in the warden service reached an all-time low due to lack of opportunity to apply their skills and to widespread public animosity. They won their spurs and the respect of the population in the Blitz. They had a surfeit of incidents then. Afterwards they reverted for a time to a programme of training and exercises, public parades, routine jobs, and an occasional social or sporting event. Better than most, they knew that other parts of the country were under frequent attack and that Jerry would return to London sooner or later. There was also dark talk of 'secret weapons' to come. So they quietly worked to improve efficiency and face whatever the future held.

The nation's fire services faced complete re-organisation in August 1941 - nationalised, in effect. Local fire brigades and the AFS merged to form the National Fire Service (NFS). The reform was introduced by Herbert Morrison, Minister of Home Security and Home Secretary, to counter administrative and technical problems that arose in the Blitz when one fire force went to the aid of another. Differences in equipment and methods between brigades had handicapped firefighting on numerous occasions. It was necessary to cut through local feelings of injured pride, resentment and jealousy when 'outsiders' appeared on the scene. The NFS did this by becoming a standardised, homogeneous organisation that achieved a complete break with the loyalties and associations of the past.

Compulsory fireguard duties were also introduced in 1941, with the lessons of the City of London in mind. In the absence of firewatchers in City offices on that fateful Sunday, fires, which could have been dealt with at an early stage by someone on the spot, were allowed to take hold before they were even spotted. The prescription for fire duty was 48 hours per month (one night a week), usually at one's place of employment, on the roof or in the upper floors, ready with buckets of sand and water and a stirrup pump, should the sirens sound. Those aged between 16 and 65 were liable for duty, unless serving part-time in the Home Guard, NFS, Women's Voluntary Service (WVS), the Civil Defence, or some other organisation recognised as useful to the war effort. Women were not excused unless they had young families to look after.

It was partly thanks to the fireguard system that, among 349 property fires in Bromley on 16-17 April 1941, over two-thirds were doused without calling for assistance from the fire services. These were early days. Had the system been fully operative, many more buildings would have been guarded.

Refugees from Nazi invaders who wished to assist had an uphill job to overcome official suspicions of their being German sympathisers planted to undermine the war effort. Jean Vollmacher, a Belgian refugee in Bromley, was in this category for nearly a year. He engaged in a bit of private firefighting at Hayes in the beginning. His first fire was at Everard Avenue, where his efforts were supervised by a policeman! Even so, he was acting illegally because under the Aliens (Movement Restriction) Order he was not supposed to leave his house after 10pm. Later he moved to 30 Mason's Hill, and in May 1941 he received official permission for volunteer firefighting. In

January 1942 he really 'arrived', being given written permission from the police "to have in his possession or under his control a bicycle". As he said, it was all in a good cause and he was proud to possess the Defence Medal in recognition of his service.

33) *London May Queen of 1941. 14-year-old Doreen Garbutt of Penge walks across Blitz debris to the cheers of her Maids of Honour and onlookers. Interesting proof of how people refused to allow the nightly bombings to upset their morale and spirit. (Kent Messenger)*

The Kentish Times said, "Despite war-time conditions, this year's May Queen Festival on Hayes Common was a charming and picturesque event." Doreen looked every inch the queen in a crinoline dress of ivory satin covered with white silk net. The crown was adorned with wild roses. In grim contrast, some local May Queens also carried gasmasks. (Quote reproduced by permission of Kentish Times Newspapers).

34) Bromley War Weapons Week. Grand Parade through the town, with the salute taken outside the town hall, 20 February 1941. Bromley set itself a target of £250,000 of new National Savings during the week, but raised £440,730. Beckenham's War Weapons Week a fortnight afterwards raised £603,968.

35) Parade of army vehicles led by a Bren Gun Carrier helping to promote Bromley's Salvage Drive, 13 September 1941. Salute taken outside the town hall in Tweedy Road. Note building with burned off roof.

36) NFS Bedford fire appliance on display at Biggin Hill air show in its original wartime livery. (Lewis Blake)

37) 52nd County of Kent Home Guard Battalion on exercise at Biggin Hill, 15 July 1942. Note NFS vehicles in the road. The Ford V8 has black out cowls fitted to the front lights and a hand-operated fire-bell attached at the side.

CHAPTER 10

Reprisal: The Nuisance Raids of 1943

Revenge, at first though sweet,
Bitter ere long back on itself recoils. (Paradise Lost)

17 January 1943: The *Luftwaffe* returned to London on this Sunday evening. It was, they said, in revenge for a strong RAF raid on Berlin the night before. Fortunately, the enemy's desire for vengeance was not equalled by his means to satisfy it. Compared with 1,500 bombers available in 1940 for operations against Britain, there were now only 250. Of these no more than 200 were serviceable on any given night. The GAF's best and most experienced aircrews were serving on the Eastern Front, while in France they were younger and untried, and there were not enough to crew even the modest number of available machines.

The night's activity came in two distinct phases. Starting at 8.30pm, the first phase lasted two hours. During this time 40 or 50 Ju88s and Do217s struggled to break through the defences to central London, but only a score got as far as the southern suburbs, where most bombs fell. Of the same number of planes (most crewed by the same men, such was the shortage of pilots) in the second phase, starting at 4.30am and lasting an hour, only ten reached the southern suburbs.

134 HE bombs were recorded in total, of which 112 fell in south London. Operating between 7,000ft - 20,000ft, the raiders constantly weaved and dived to evade the worst of the flak, illumination by searchlights, or a lethal encounter with an RAF Beaufighter.

For the population at large, denied their beds and somewhat out of condition in regard to air raids, the most disturbing thing was the debut of London's greatly improved AA defences. Crashing and thudding gunfire exceeded anything remembered from the Blitz. It was not so much a matter of more guns but the remarkably rapid rate of fire achieved using a new fuse-setter invented and manufactured by Molins of Deptford. Moreover, Londoners got a first taste of massed firings of AA rockets (UPs - unrotated projectiles). These hurtled skywards simultaneously at 1,000mph in a mad rush and roar, then exploded together in a mighty thundercrash. Some voices whispered that the raid on Berlin had been made only to provoke retaliation on London in order its new defences might be tested out!

Teething troubles with a new mechanical fuse led to many AA shells falling back to ground. Among eight people reported killed in London by this 'friendly fire' was PC Robert Burns of Chelsea police station who was staying with friends at 156 London Lane, Bromley. While he stood in the doorway watching the immense display of AA fireworks, a shell exploded in the road and struck him down. Another policeman was reported seriously injured by a shell in Court Road, Orpington. Special Constable John Jelf was among 34 people injured from this cause.

Bombs fell across a wide swathe of SE London, all around Bromley, west, north, and east - from Purley and Coulsdon to Old Bexley and Crayford, through Addington Village, Brockley, Greenwich, Charlton, Eltham, Woolwich and Plumstead - but by some stroke of luck they missed the Bromley area entirely. Seventy lives were lost, twenty in Brockley alone. Two large and 53 other fires were started - mostly by new incendiary weapons, viz., large containers (AB500 and AB1000 releasing hundreds of IBs at one go) and the *Sprengbrand* (explosive firebomb) which the ARP called 'firepots'. A serious fire broke out at Jones and Higgins in Peckham, a department store well-known to Bromley residents.

A Ministry of Home Security bulletin declared that "the GAF fulfilled the threat of reprisals, put out from Rome, by bombing London. It was a weak reply and the bombers were roughly handled. Suburbs in south London received the main force of the attacks". One Beaufighter crew alone accounted for three raiders - Ju88s brought down at Brenzett, Kent and at Caterham, and a Do217 at Westerham.

Although the raiders' reports tried to put a good gloss on it, German leaders were displeased with the night's work; it entirely lacked the salutary lesson desired of it in Berlin; Goering's *Luftwaffe* suffered further loss of face in the German High Command's estimation. Some kind of sequel was sought to rehabilitate it and placate indignant Berliners... something different, with an element of surprise....

20 January 1943: Settled weather with cloud cover on this Wednesday offered ideal conditions for what the GAF had in mind - a surprise, low-level attack in force in broad daylight on the capital, a venture never attempted before, even in 1940. At 12.25pm a force of 28 fast FW190s roared across Romney Marsh at zero feet, the majority armed with a single 500kg or 250kg bomb, but several almost certainly acting as fighter escorts on the right (east) flank. Covering the FW190s' west flank was an escort of 60 Me109s, which crossed the coast between Hastings and Beachy Head. A diversionary sweep by Me109s off North Foreland was designed to draw RAF fighters away from where they would be needed.

At this period of the war a low-level incursion of this nature in broad daylight would be assumed by the defenders as directed against an undefended coastal resort or town near the coast. It was happening all the time, albeit not on this scale as yet. Doubtless the RAF and the ROC were wrong-footed by such expectation in this instance, hence failed to recognise in good time that London was the target. Even the trained interpreter may see only what he expects to see! This has never been given as a factor in the failure to warn London of the impending attack, but it seems highly plausible, especially when six breakaway raiders turning east were immediately taken as the main force heading for Maidstone. They might simply have been FW190 escorts in fighter mode breaking off to return to base.

Unspecified equipment failures were also given as reasons for the ROC 'losing the plot'- in more senses than one - though it was then the RAF's task to interpret ROC reports and issue public warnings as appropriate.

As FW190s swept over the North Downs, the defenders still could not bring themselves to believe London would be the target of a raid of this type. It was simply unheard of, even in the Battle of Britain. So only in the outer suburbs of Bromley, Beckenham, Penge, etc., were sirens sounded - just moments before the raiders roared across rooftops *en route* for Catford, Deptford, Rotherhithe, Greenwich and Poplar.

This was the occasion of the notorious bombing of Sandhurst Road School, Catford, in which six teachers and 38 children lost their lives. Among the dead was Ethel Betts, head of the junior department, who lived in Bird-in-Hand Lane, Bickley, and several children whose homes had Bromley or Beckenham postal addresses.

London's balloons were caught on the ground by the speed of events, becoming easy targets for machine-gunning as the raiders flew over. Six persons were injured by MG fire in Hawthorn Grove and Crampton Road, Penge, probably in a long strafing run-up to the balloon at Maybourne, Springfield Road, Sydenham, which was set ablaze along with a timber-built barrack room. The balloon in Copers Cope Road, Beckenham was also strafed and destroyed by fire, with two injuries reported. Turning west and south after releasing their bombs, some raiders gave short bursts of fire on their way out. The *Paxton Arms*, Anerley Hill was hit by cannon shells, the marks said to be visible still; locomotives at Norwood Junction were also hit.

A fire at Bell Green gasworks, previously thought to be due to MG fire, may have been started by light AA shells, a burst of which damaged Haseltine Road School and houses in the vicinity. One imagines gun barrels were depressed low in order to hit the rooftop raiders and that some rounds struck buildings in the line of fire.

LAA guns near Dorking evidently had a clearer field of fire - they damaged and caused to crash at Capel one FW190 fleeing the country. Having fallen behind the main force on the inward flight over the Channel, the pilot told his captors that he jettisoned his bomb in the sea so as to catch up and act as a fighter escort. A small point, perhaps, but one which lends credence to the idea of FW190 escorts being among the force. However that may be, it seems there was this free-lance flyer over London, 'doing his own thing', as well as 22 FW190s carrying bombs.

Claims sometimes made that Biggin Hill airfield, not London, was the intended target are not borne out by the evidence. The Station's Operations Book for 20 January states: "The Abbeville Boys visited Biggin Hill for a change, at about 1415 hours (sic.) they came in low over the coast and flew round the aerodrome perimeter."

'Abbeville' refers to the main base of FW190 fighter-bombers then plaguing England's south and east coasts and which RAF fighters frequently 'visited' on strafing attacks. 'Flying round the perimeter' did not mean circling the airfield. The line of flight took the raiders past the airfield, but two miles to the east over Cudham and Downe. Close enough, as it happens, for the airfield's machine-gunners to think it worthwhile to expend 1,100 rounds of .303 ammunition on them as they flashed by, undeflected from their purpose and probably unaware they were being fired at.

Nocturnal air raid alarms became a regular feature of 1943 for London's southern and eastern boroughs. Most attacks were justifiably dubbed 'nuisance raids', carried out by single marauders or small groups hoping to get a lucky hit on something of consequence before beating a hasty retreat back to base. It was not unknown, however, for such nuisances to produce a large number of casualties. Occasionally, the GAF mounted a more serious force, which would precipitate a very lively and noisy confrontation over the suburbs.

3-4 March 1943: The night witnessed two raids of some strength. Alerts lasted between 8.15pm-9.45pm and 4am-5am, with an estimated ten aircraft reaching the capital each time. Approach was from ENE, which left SE London relatively untouched on the southern flank. AA gunners excelled themselves in the sheer weight of metal and explosive propelled skywards - 12,316 heavy shells and 2,496 rockets, of which 308 and 35 respectively fell back to earth. In reply the raiders managed a mere 74 HEs on target.

Bromley's share of the bombardment emanated solely as friendly fire - 24 HAA shells and four UPs. The only fatality is believed to have been a horse in Main Road, Knockholt, but a number of homes were damaged in Padua and Kingsdale Roads, Penge. It was during this raid that men drawn from the 52nd, 53rd and 54th County of Kent HG Battalions first went into action with 3.7inch AA guns at Thornet Wood, Bromley.

24 April 1943: The Ju88 approaching Bromley at midnight on this stormy Easter Weekend was untroubled by guns, which should have made the crew very wary of night fighters. The plane had been plotted by the ROC for more

38) 12.35pm. Wednesday, 20 January 1943. An impression of eight low-level FW190s flying over Bromley Road/ Bellingham Road before bombing Catford. 14 others passed over Beckenham and Penge before attacking Deptford and Rotherhithe. (Lewis Blake)

than an hour flying aimlessly over the south Midlands, before turning on a south-easterly course.

As far as the Mosquito crew of No. 85 Squadron, based at Hunsdon, Hertfordshire were concerned, the visitor had long outstayed his welcome. The duty team at Bromley ROC Centre watched with interest when the plots of the Mosquito and its unsuspecting prey drew together as they approached at 3,000ft. The last act in this drama appeared likely to occur almost overhead, so they stepped out into the blustery night to see what happened. Sure enough, a sharp rattle of cannon fire echoed across the town's blacked out streets and flames appeared in the sky. Moments later the sky lit up in a vivid pink and white flash, followed by an immense thunderclap, enough to waken the soundest sleeper.

Wreckage spewed from above in a series of heavy bangs and thuds in and around Widmore Road-Plaistow Lane. Most consisted of chunks of twisted metal, wheels, guns, engine parts, and the like. Some pieces fell in the garden of 118 Widmore Road, for many years a maternity home. A fire was started at Bromley Cricket Club, but the main damage was at 124-126 Widmore Road, where exploding ammunition set fire to both 14-room detached houses.

Raymond Wattenbach, then a pupil at Bickley Hall School, cycled round the area on Sunday morning to discover what he could of the violent explosion.

According to what he remembered, the scout hall opposite Bromley Cricket Club was burned down by one of the engines. The body of one crew member was found close by. Someone told him it lay with arms and legs presenting the shape of a swastika. In the cricket ground he saw the cockpit near the pavilion. Since no one guarded it, he recovered one or two souvenirs - standard schoolboys' practice at the time. Through the roof of a house near Holy Trinity Convent a wing pointed to the sky. A cannon lay in Homefield Road, junction with Widmore Road, and other wreckage was guarded by a member of the RAF Regiment on the corner of Plaistow Lane and Homefield Road.

Only one member of the crew survived the encounter. He was found in a nearby street staggering in a daze and taken to a warden's post. He had baled out just before the plane exploded. Of the remaining crew, two bodies were found in fields and the third by an aircraft engine.

Intriguing questions arise about this incident. What was the plane doing flying aimlessly over the English countryside for so long? Why did it fly across London at only 3,000ft., exposing itself to close-range ack-ack and high risk of collision with barrage balloon cables? Why was it left to its own devices for so long?

The affair had all the hallmarks of RAF *Meaconing*. This was the system of masking radio beacons in France (which German pilots used for navigating home when lost or unsure of their position) by radiating identical signals from beacons in England. Disorientated pilots would fly from one English beacon to another thinking they were over France but not seeing the expected landing lights. They ran out of fuel and crashed, landed on a British airfield in error, or wandered out to sea and were never heard of again.

The first operational Meacon station was established at Flimwell, off the A21 Hastings Road near Tunbridge Wells. Is it possible that the ill-fated Ju88 was being *Meaconed* by Flimwell? The pilot never found out. Neither shall we now, but it was certainly on the appropriate bearing.

Bomb incidents were relatively rare in the spring and summer of 1943, despite fairly frequent soundings of warning sirens and the noise of gunfire - sometimes close, sometimes just a distant rumbling.

18 May: 1.44am. Houses damaged in Skeet Hill Lane, Orpington.
6 June: 2am. HEs and PhIBs (phosphorous incendiary bombs) struck Beckenham in Durban, Cedars, Cromwell, and Hampden roads, killing a young woman at 43 Cedars Road, which was destroyed, and fatally injuring a man at 64 Durban Road.

23 June: In the early hours four people injured in Monks Orchard Road/ Pine Avenue, Beckenham. At Sidcup one person was killed and two injured in Parsonage Lane.

Dr Goebbels, the German Propaganda Minister, recorded, "The London public fears that a German air Blitzkrieg will suddenly break out again overnight. Would to God that we were in a position to do it! Obviously the English people consider us to be better armed than we actually are."

9 July: Afternoon. 10 raiders crossed the south coast in low cloud and two Do217s penetrated as far as Croydon, dropping 500kg HEs on Thornton Heath and Addiscombe with the loss of at least nine lives. Ten HEs were also recorded at Biggin Hill, with no reported casualties. One Do217 was attacked by a fighter over Banstead and Wallington and again over South Croydon, after having carried out its attack. The plane crashed at Bletchingley and was claimed by gunners at Kenley airfield.

7 October: A sharp evening attack. About 60 planes were involved, mostly Ju88s. The bombing was confined to southern and eastern suburbs. The raiders flew fast and high and took sharp evasive action when engaged by AA guns. Searchlights illuminated and coned targets as high as 25,000ft, but the gunners did not make the most of their opportunities. Even the uninitiated on the ground who stood to watch remarked on the flak's inaccuracy, perhaps induced by the Germans' first use of *Dueppel* to confuse AA radars. Already used by the RAF on Hamburg with disastrous results for that city, *Window*, as it was called in Britain, comprised thin strips of aluminium foil dropped in bundles which cluttered radar screens with false signals. It's now called *Chaff.*

Central Bromley was hit by a string of HEs. A direct hit on Bromley South Station killed three and injured eighteen. Another hit a nursery school in Holwood Road. In Elmfield Road a 20,000 gallon emergency water supply reservoir was blown up. An HE outside Dolcis shoe store in the High Street killed Harry Evans of 30 Aylesbury Road; the shop front was wrecked and 34 other shops damaged by the blast. 41 Aylesbury Road was demolished in another incident, and one person lost his life at 34 Bromley Gardens. In Hayes Way, Beckenham several houses were destroyed.

The *Bromley Times* (15-10-1943) mentioned "... a bomb near a shoe shop wrecked the front and damaged stores on both sides of the road. Lower down the street a cycle shop was destroyed and an ATS girl was killed while sheltering in the doorway. Mr T. W. Munks, a firewatcher, was also killed; his wife and family escaped injury though badly shocked." No mention here of the station, because the censor did not permit disclosure of damage to the railway system.

Mrs Diament of Barnet was on the platform at Bromley South when it was hit. Her husband pushed her to the ground just in time to save her from the fate of a woman standing alongside who was killed under a hail of bomb fragments. Mrs Diament was slightly cut. She said the injured sat in the booking hall for what seemed like ages waiting for treatment.

A gentleman from South Drive, Orpington was angered by what he witnessed at the station and wrote a letter of complaint to the Home Office:

> "I have never seen a more disgraceful scene...A crowd of twenty wardens were there but there was no first aid party and no first aid equipment available. Men lacked first aid knowledge and borrowed handkerchiefs for bandages. A man with a severed foot had a handkerchief tied round the upper part of the leg which did not prevent the bleeding. Nothing was done to arrest the bleeding of a chest wound. Someone cut open his shirt, took a look, and closed the shirt again. No bandages, no nothing....The ambulance took 45 minutes to arrive... No one seemed to be in charge. All the wardens did was walk about...."

A senior CD officer looked into the matter. He reported that Dr Tapper, Bromley's MoH, had been occupied attending casualties outside Dolcis. Dr. Tapper then went to the station, where in his opinion the first aid was excellent. An army medical officer happened to be on the station and treated the casualty with the badly injured foot as best he could without first aid equipment. Dr Tapper was said to be at a loss to understand the accusations, although with the station blacked out and crowded there might have been initial difficulties. Bromley Hospital said they were satisfied with the first aid, and a Southern Railway superintendent at the scene considered the Civil Defence "able and orderly".

It was admitted the ambulance had been delayed. This was due to the driver mistakenly going to the High Street incidents after being told by policemen that she was at Bromley South. Thereupon she helped ambulance crews already in the High Street. The bombs fell at 8.55pm. Light rescue units arrived at the station at 9.18pm. The ambulance finally arrived at the station 9.34pm. All the injured needing hospital treatment were in Bromley's casualty ward by 9.50pm.

The details are given here because they illustrate the difficulties faced by the emergency services in the black out during an air raid. Some suspicion of incompetence remains. The letter writer was apparently right about lack of first aid equipment, which seems strange at a busy railway station and with a FAP two hundred yards away in Mason's Hill. And surely a local ambulance driver should have known where to find Bromley South station. It was only two minutes walk from the hospital. The CD officer ended his report by opining that, ".... some of the CD personnel seemed rather shaken by what had been a sharp and unpleasant form of attack."

20-21 October: Ju88s, FW190s, and Me410s made a determined effort to bomb central London. Most progressed no farther than the outer suburbs, where the raid broke up in an orgy of shells, tracers, swaying searchlights, flares, and rockets. Somewhere in this chaos of sound and light aircraft could be heard or, shining like silver fish, were seen coned by searchlights and under unremitting AA fire.

It was bad news for people on the ground nearby when a bomber was coned by searchlights. A raider caught this way over Sidcup at 1am was quickly hit by gunfire and just as quickly unloaded a 500kg HE on Old Farm Avenue; a direct hit on Nos. 21-25, which led to seven deaths and 17 injuries. Because residents reported strange lights and sparks in the sky, the Ministry of Home Security sent someone to look into the matter. He concluded that what had been seen were burning parts of the plane, a view confirmed by pieces of light alloy of German make found in Lamorbey Park. Bromley ROC reported that the plane was last plotted leaving the country thirty miles east of Maidstone, at 1,000ft and evidently in trouble. Two FW190s failed to return to base, so it is likely the Sidcup bomber was lost in the cold waters of the North Sea.

22 October: 7.30pm. Anglesea Road, St Mary Cray hit by one or more HEs among a score in the Orpington area. D/H on houses killed seven residents and injured sixteen at Nos. 64-66. Fatalities included John Petty and his wife, Edith, both aged 47, and Special Constable John Russ aged 60, and his wife, Daisy, 53. Three houses were destroyed and 80 badly damaged.

With further minor visitations on subsequent nights, Bromley was under alert for eight nights out of eleven. Nearly all the one hundred serious casualties in London relating to these attacks occurred in south eastern suburbs. The first week of November was much the same - every night an alert, usually triggered by a few isolated raiders who seldom had much to show for their efforts. However, one could never tell what might occur.

7 November: Only three aircraft flew over London, yet a D/H on the Cinderella Dance Hall in Putney High Street killed 72 and seriously injured 115 youngsters who crowded the dance floor or were milling about the street without regard to the warning sirens and sounds of gunfire. The dance band was virtually wiped out and nothing but shoes and pieces of their clothing were ever found.

In Beckenham a heavy bomb demolished 132-134 Victor Road, killing or injuring eight people. Kathleen Hawkes, aged 32, and her children, Jean, 10 and John, 4 died at No. 132. David Johnson, a close friend of the Hawkes family, described Jean as a good-looking girl with a lovely personality. Her tenth birthday party was held earlier in the evening of the night she was killed. Jean and David's sister, Valerie, were the best of friends. After the bomb fell and the AA fire decreased people emerged from their shelters to the sounds of fire engines and ARP voices. David's sister suddenly screamed, *Jean, Jean, Jean!* David managed to dodge his parents' control and rushed to the end of the road.... Huge flames were leaping in the air... There seemed little hope.... But for Valerie's sake they kept the thought to themselves.

A fourth fatality was a Mr Wilson. After returning from a Salvation Army meeting in Penge and still in uniform, he had gone to keep the Hawkes company at the start of the raid - Mrs Hawkes' husband was a PoW in Japanese hands. David said in a letter to the present writer, " I heard only in 1992 that Mr Wilson's body showed no marks and other than dust his uniform was perfect. I hope the Hawkes did not show signs of a painful death. I dared not enquire. I was 13 years of age at the time... A tear is still shed for these innocent victims."

The RAF commented that since March no night reprisal raids had been made for the devastating bombing of Germany. ".... such attacks as have been made have shown either a deplorable state of navigational training or a distinct reluctance of crews to press home attacks..." It was true - *Luftwaffe* bomber crews were seldom prepared to persevere against strong opposition. RAF Bomber Command was in an altogether different class. Just as well for the British people it was not the other way round.

39) *Wreckage of a Ju88 collected behind Holy Trinity Convent, Plaistow Lane, 24 April 1943. Cannon fire by an RAF Mosquito of 85 Squadron caused the aircraft explode over Bickley in "a vivid pink and white flash".*

40) A view of Anglesea Road c.1900 giving a pre-war view of the houses behind the cruel and bizarre spectacle of a dancing bear, drawing a sizable crowd.

41) A direct hit on houses in Anglesea Road, St Mary Cray on the evening of 22 October 1943 killed or injured 24 people. Extensive re-building was needed after the war. (Lewis Blake)

42) Men of 54th County of Kent Home Guard Battalion inspected by Col. F.W. Chamberlain on a raw winter's morning at West Wickham Cricket Club. Men from this and other local HG units manned 3.7inch AA guns at nights in 1943-1944 - at Thornet Wood, Bromley for example; fatiguing work after a day at one's full-time job.

CHAPTER 11

Steinbock - The Mountain Wild Goat

The crimson flower of battle blooms,
And solemn marches fill the nights. (Julia Ward Howe)

1943 ended on a subdued note, which was not at all what the GAF had planned. Goaded beyond endurance by the RAF's calamitous bombings of the Fatherland, Reichmarshall Hermann Goering ordered in reinforcements for another attempt to intensify the air war, "To avenge the terror attacks by the enemy". The new campaign, Operation *Steinbock* (ibex or mountain wild goat), was planned to start in mid-December 1943 but bad weather delayed it until the third week of January 1944. Originally the Germans had intended to combine the aerial offensive on London with salvoes of V1 flying bombs, but operational deployment of this weapon had fallen so far behind schedule that *Steinbock* went ahead with piloted aircraft only.

An assembly of some 450-500 serviceable bombers in occupied Europe stood ready in January waiting for weather conditions to improve. About 50% were Ju88s, 20% were Do217s, and the remainder were made up of Ju188s, Me410s, FW190s, and He177s (4-engine planes able to carry a seven-ton bomb load but unreliable and dangerous to fly). It was quite a powerful assembly on paper and capable theoretically on a 'maximum effort' of delivering in the order of 800 tons of high explosives and incendiaries. The Eastern Front and the Mediterranean theatre had been scoured for spare planes and crews to make up the numbers and so far as piloted bombing of Britain was concerned, 'Ibex, the mountain wild goat' was effectively the last shot in the GAF's locker. No replacements could be spared for crews lost. All further 'terror reprisals' would rely on V1 flying bombs or V2 rockets.

The first night of the offensive, which the British dubbed 'Baby Blitz' or 'Little Blitz', was 21-22 January. Before then isolated raiders came over on several nights. On the 2nd two 250kg HEs in Wren Road, Sidcup damaged 120 houses and injured twelve people, and at Hayes there was a direct hit on 38 Hilldown Road and one person reported killed in Tiepigs Lane. Subsequent nights produced incidents on Kangley Bridge Industrial Estate, Sydenham, and direct hits on the Davis Theatre and Allders department store in Croydon.

21-22 January: 450 sorties divided into two phases at 8.49pm- 10.10pm and 4.29am-5.45am made this the heaviest night's activity over London and SE England since May 1941. A combination of unexpected poor weather over England, aircrew inexperience, some dubious target marking, a heavy barrage of AA fire, and British radio counter-measures threw the whole operation into disarray. Only a handful of raiders located their sprawling target and of just 32 tons of bombs on London, nearly all fell south of the river. AA gunners had a field day - or night - pounding the sky with a record 33,824 heavy shells, about 300 per minute/target engagement. Fewer than twenty lives were lost in London but the shattering din of gunfire made it all seem much worse.

Main incidents locally were numerous house fires in Rangefield, Farmfield and Headcorn roads, Downham; some 1,000 IBs, including 200 UX, in the Burnt Ash Lane area; casualties in Stodart Road, Penge; bombs in the grounds of Orpington Hospital, no one hurt; ten houses set on fire in Birkbeck and Ravenscroft roads, Beckenham; a severe fire at Lamorbey Park Hotel, Sidcup; and many house fires just across the border with Sydenham in Newlands Park, Trewsbury Road, etc.

The GAF appears to have lost at least 20 planes in the night's débâcle, including four victims of AA fire, which later crashed at Dover, Billericay, Canterbury, and in the Channel off Worthing.

29-30 January: The second big raid of the offensive had London again as the target. About 100 aircraft crossed the coast but only 20-25 reached the capital. Three times more bombs fell on Kent and Essex than on London, though two-thirds of all serious casualties were in the London Region - some 120 out of 180. The raid was notable for the first use of 1,000kg parachute-stabilised HEs, two of which blew up in Oakdene Road, St Mary Cray, damaging many homes, without report of serious casualties.

3-4 February: This night witnessed a double raid on London at 8.40pm-9.20pm and 4.25am-6.10am. 80 bombers and 15 fighter-bombers were plotted overland, yet only five found the metropolis in the first phase and twelve in the second. Weight of bombs on London was reckoned at 26 tons. 33 people were killed in south east England, about one half in the London area.

Bromley and Chislehurst recorded 1,400 IBs and ten 50kg PhIBs. These started 110 fires but due to prompt action by fireguards only three required attendance by NFS units. One of them was at Walden Manor in Walden Road, Chislehurst, a 40-room mansion in use by Harrison Gibson's department store for furniture storage. A severe blaze took hold on the top floor and the roof was burned off. At the same time in Whitehorse Hill, one of Coldharbour Cottages was set ablaze.

Two fatalities were reported in Mottingham and Sidcup (at 259 Dunkery Road and 91 Halfway Street), likely to have been victims of explosive IBs which would burn for some minutes before detonating and killing any unsuspecting person who approached near. In Bromley itself the largest single cluster of fires severely damaged thirteen houses in the area of

Avondale Road, King's Avenue, Plaistow Lane, etc.

13-14 February: After several nights of minor activity, the GAF claimed to have mustered 240 bomber sorties against England on this occasion. However, only 100 aircraft were plotted crossing the coast (between Orfordness and North Foreland), and only 15 found their way to London. Every night the story was the same: either one side was exaggerating for propaganda purposes or someone couldn't count. Judging by the poor results, it rather seemed the exaggerations emanated from Berlin.

Only four tons of HE and a prominent use of incendiaries were reported in the London Region. Walden Farm at St Mary Cray received the full contents of an AB1000 canister - some 600-700 IBs in all, which burned out harmlessly. The night's work cost the enemy eight aircraft: two Ju88s shot down by Mosquitos, one near Romford, the other two miles south of Whitstable; six others simply went missing or crashed on the way back to base.

18-19 February: For the first time since *Steinbock* started, the bombers successfully concentrated their attack on central London and began making for a time some real impact. The change was part result of growing experience, part careful attention to route and target marking and part a severe upbraiding by *Luftwaffe* leaders of the crews on their lamentable performance so far. By the same token outer suburbs had much less to report in the way of incidents.

The official war history, *Defence of the UK*, speaks of this night's activity as the heaviest actual bombing of the capital since 10 May 1941 - 200 sorties, 120 enemy aircraft plotted overland, 139 tons of HE on target, over 500 fires started, 180 Londoners killed and 300 seriously injured.

For the Bromley area the significant incident was a severe blaze in another 40-room mansion in Chislehurst, namely, Camden Place Golf Club-house. Staff and residents could not cope with the 50 or 60 firebombs which came through the roof. Fierce flames drove them downstairs and much of the premises was left charred and burnt out. The ground floor dining room was destroyed and with it fine panelling and tapestries.

20-21 February: The attack on this Sunday occurred in the late evening, reaching a peak at 10pm-10.30pm. It was about the same strength as that two nights previously, with the same total bomb load hitting the target. 600 fires broke out and the London death toll climbed to 218. One force of raiders approached from the north-east and a second via the Thames Estuary and north Kent, but most of the bombing was targeted on central districts. Target flares were laid out across outer boroughs in SE London indicating the start of some bomb runs, and large numbers of IBs were shown to have fallen on the southern margins of the region. Little is known about the effects of these IBs, so presumably they did little harm to life or property.

Most raiders returned to their bases on a south-easterly course across Bromley and adjoining districts, heading in a slow descent for clusters of yellow flares over the Godstone-Westerham area which pointed them in the right direction. Searchlights and heavy gunfire harried them all the way. People held their breath as they passed over, not knowing that their bomb racks were now empty. It was at this point that a Ju88 in the general retreat was hit by local AA fire and crashed near Selhurst station.

22-23 February: A concentrated 15-minute raid at 3am by an estimated 50 bombers over London failed to produce incidents of particular note in outer south-eastern suburbs. Most of the damage occurred in west and east London and was caused by nearly 250 fires. Aging Ju88s continued to offer the best pickings for the defences - three were shot down. Heavy guns scored notable successes in bringing down one each of the newer, faster Me410s and Ju188s. Another Me410 fell to a Mosquito in Sussex. Most useful was the destruction by a Mosquito of a He177 over Suffolk. Two FW190s also failed to return from the night's operations.

23-24 February: Attacks on London had certainly been carrying a heavier punch in recent nights, and this night was no exception. In a 30-minute period during the late evening some 90 aircraft dropped 100+ tons of HEs and IBs spread over half the capital's boroughs and suburbs. Casualties approached 200 killed and 350 seriously injured. The GAF had learned from Bomber Command the value of compressing raids into the shortest possible time, thereby increasing the chances of swamping the defences whilst reducing their opportunity to pick off planes at leisure.

In Beckenham at 10.45pm ten separate fires severely damaged 40 homes; at 72-74 Goodhart Way, 186-200 Langley Way, 261-263 Pickhurst Rise, etc., and set fire to the rail track between Hayes and West Wickham stations. Concentrations of fires in this manner resulted from the enemy's use of AB500 and AB1000 IB containers, which - if they worked properly - released hundreds of firebombs in layers during the canister's descent. It was a frightening business to be caught in such a cascade, surrounded by a rapid sequence of vivid flashes and firecracker explosions. Woe betide anyone in an upstairs bedroom if one or more fell through the roof.

A container in this raid which had failed to discharge its bombs crashed through to the ground floor of 10a Thicket Road and engulfed the house in a mass of flames. Local fireguards could not cope and called in the NFS. One fireguard, Hilda Arnold aged 45, died from her injuries next day in Beckenham Hospital.

More often than not during the Baby Blitz deaths or injuries suffered by Civil Defence personnel were due to the presence of IBSENs in AB500 and AB1000 containers. The letters stood for 'incendiary bomb with separating explosive nose'. It was in effect a firebomb and a small HE device combined which separated on impact. The IB element ignited, while the HE part, whose presence some feet or yards away might not be noticed, was designed to explode minutes later. This was without question an anti-personnel device intended to maim or kill anyone who attempted to extinguish fires, although it also served to spread flames by blasting burning material far and wide. An example in this raid was at a major fire in the Victoria Laundry, Croydon, where two watchmen were killed by IBSENs; they had been "too enthusiastic in tackling them".

Numerous fires were also started in Penge, Keston, and Sidcup. Elsewhere, isolated farms were not spared. 700 firebombs fell in a deluge on North End Farm, Downe, setting light to the farmhouse and outbuildings and burning livestock to death. The farm's 'stirrup pump squad' dealt with the farmhouse blaze while the NFS concentrated on the outbuildings.

It was not a particularly good night for the defences. Two or three Ju88s went missing or crashed during their return flight, otherwise a Do217 was hit by HAA over west London. After the crew baled out, the plane flew on for sixty miles before performing, without human assistance, a reasonably good belly landing on vegetable allotments at Cambridge.

24-25 February: Here they were - back again, six nights out of seven! Things seemed to be getting like the 1940 Blitz of old. But there were important differences, such as the short time the enemy spent over the target, his greater reliance on incendiarism, high failure rates in reaching the target, and high loss rates in men and machines (seldom less than 5% of sorties flown, and usually more).

The GAF believed in trying new routes to the capital in the hope of finding a gap in the defensive lines or deceiving the defenders about their intentions. They tried an unusually circuitous route this time. Alfred Price in *Blitz on Britain* records that the raiders flew north to High Wycombe, turned on red markers, then flew south east to bomb west and SW London before flying out over SE suburbs in a shallow descent. It was almost certainly a tactical mistake, for it presented a more difficult navigational task to flyers who found the most direct routes testing enough, and it gave night-fighters more time to ambush them on the way in and again on the way home.

Six of their number were shot down by Mosquitos over Kent, Surrey, and Sussex. At least three more were lost to RAF intruders on the French side or disappeared in uncertain circumstances. With perhaps 90 or so aircraft plotted crossing the coast (against 170 sorties claimed by the Germans), this represented a loss rate in the region of 10 per cent - unsustainable for long even were adequate replacements available and the flyers were not badly needed elsewhere.

1-2 March: Some minor scattered bombing on 29 February produced blast damage to 80 houses and H. J. Maybrey's aluminium alloy castings works in

Worsley Bridge Road, just inside Beckenham's border. The next night witnessed a substantial raid involving SE London, which the Ministry of Home Security dismissed as "a poor effort" and "ineffective". Whitehall generally took this view when central and west London were not affected. There were at any rate 105 fires in the area, some quite serious, like those at Goldsmiths' College, Siemens Bros. cable works, and RAF Kidbrooke. Casualties, however, were light at 15-20 killed.

The raid took place between 2.40am and 3.37am. At 3am cascades of IBs set fire to and severely damaged 'Cranmore' in Walden Road, Chislehurst (a 35 room house) and 'Sitka' in Southill Road (40 room house). Both roofs were burned off, and four NFS men were injured tackling the fires.

14-15 March: For the first time in two weeks raiders returned to London in significant numbers between 10.30pm and midnight. An estimated 50- 60 bombers penetrated as far as the metropolis, where they caused 400 fires requiring attendance by the NFS. Nearly all boroughs were affected to some extent, but the figure for fatalities was modest at 25, of which at least five were in Bromley.

A 500kg HE killed two at 78-80 Widmore Road, Bromley, including four-year-old Fenella Rogers-Lewis. Other HEs fell in Murray Avenue and Thornton Road, the latter causing fire and blast damage to Westminster School sports pavilion. Three persons died at 16 Ash Tree Way, West Wickham, including a 17-month old baby. A one-ton bomb, which struck Elmers End, fortunately missed nearby houses to fall on allotments at the rear of Ancaster Road.

The *Luftwaffe* paid a steep price for this attack. Ten Ju88s, a Ju188, two Do 217s, and two FW190s were shot down, crashed on their return flight, or went missing. Not for the first time, more enemy airmen were probably killed than people on the ground.

21-22 March: After a few nights' comparative rest in which to ponder on what it was achieving and at what cost, the GAF turned its attentions to Hull on 19-20 March, or so German sources claimed. Either the crews were not told of the target or they had their own ideas about what they should bomb. Some 90 tons of explosives were spread over East Anglia and Lincolnshire, but none fell on Hull.

On 21-22nd the GAF resumed the Baby Blitz on London. The alert lasted from 0.44am till 1.56am, with actual bombing compressed into a half-hour period between 1am and 1.30am. One body of enemy aircraft crossed the east coast and bombed areas in east and north London; a second force attacked from Kent and Sussex, concentrating on SE London.
It was the worst night of the Baby Blitz for the boroughs of Lewisham, Greenwich, and Deptford. The Bromley area also had a share of incidents.

Among these were HE bombs in Eastbury Road and Towncourt Lane, Petts Wood, in which nine houses were destroyed, one person was killed and about 30 injured. Then at 'Del-cyl' in Chislehurst Road a heavy HE claimed two lives. A full container of IBs struck a children's nursery, which the NFS were able to save, despite extensive fire damage. Nurses were reported as having rescued babies by carrying them out through a first floor window and down a tree to the ground.

A severe fire raged at an army vehicle park in Gates Green Road, West Wickham. Army lorries, Bofors trailers, and a marquee were destroyed, along with substantial fire damage to No. 137, which was in use by the military. The flames proved beyond the resources of army fireguards and the NFS were called upon to assist.

A 20-year-old woman was killed at 'The Dell', Hartfield Crescent, Beckenham, and fires severely damaged houses at 100, 118 and 243 Upper Elmers End Road and 47 Stone Park Avenue. In Orpington a house burned to the ground when an HE blasted coals from a domestic fire across one of the rooms. A particular tragedy occurred at the Old Rectory, Knockholt, which suffered a direct hit by a full IB container. The front of the house caught fire immediately, and the Revd. Charles Hobley, aged 84, who served as an ARP warden, was trapped and burned to death in his indoor Morrison shelter before rescuers could reach him. Several firemen were injured in fighting the blaze.

Altogether, 40 people were killed and 225 injured in London. 90 tons of HEs and IBs came down on the capital and its southern outskirts, with the usual preponderance of incendiaries. Of 722 fires in total, 496 were in south east boroughs, including nearly all the 99 that required attendance by the NFS. Ten bombers were shot down or otherwise failed to return to base - about 11 per cent of the number plotted overland.

24-25 March: Of the fifteen **major** raids in the *Steinbock* offensive, thirteen were directed against London and the penultimate attack of any great consequence came on this night. It also happened to be the worst attack for the Bromley area, Croydon, and West Norwood. The alert lasted from 10.54pm till 0.58am in London's central warning zone, and 10.53pm-0.59am in the southern suburbs. 60 aircraft operated over London south of the river. "Damage was not commensurate with the scale of effort", according to one official account, but that depended on where you were sitting.

Penge:
- 0.03am. HEs completely destroyed Holy Trinity Church, Penge, and 226-228 Anerley Road. Nos. 230-232 and 205-215 were badly damaged. One person was killed at No. 228. There were 15 injuries.
- 0.05am. HE and PhIBs severely damaged by fire and blast the Co-op furniture store in Franklin Road.

- 0.06am. HEs in Kenilworth Road damaged Nos. 38-46 and 35-39. Four people injured. IBs in Hawthorne Road led to the gutting of two houses; one person died and five were injured. PhIB in Selby Road injured two.

Hayes:
- 0.15am. Area struck by four AB1000s containing a mix of IBs and IBSENs. Serious fires in Station Approach included Barclays Bank, a café (McKechnie's), David Greig (multiple grocers), Rumsey's (chemist), and the post office. Pamela Mote, aged 4, was killed in the flat above Barclays Bank. Patricia Crowhurst, aged 6, lost her life above Rumsey's. Nearby houses were also set alight, including 68-78 West Common Road, three houses in Grove Road, and a severe blaze at 11 Hayes Gardens.

Beckenham:
- 0.15am. More than 60 properties burned together in and around Birkbeck and Mackenzie roads when the district was saturated by the contents of IB containers. The situation was categorised by the NFS as a 'fire zone', which indicated an urgent call for every available unit to attend in order to contain what might develop into an area conflagration.

34 houses and flats in Birkbeck Road were well alight when the first NFS appliances arrived on the scene (Nos. 105-109 and 115-133 were very badly damaged; nos. 139-163, 171, 183, and 132-134 suffered substantial damage); also 18 properties in Mackenzie Road (Nos. 119, 135, and 165 severely damaged); and six properties in Avenue Road, including No. 86 - T. Wall & Son, ice cream merchants, with roof and top floor destroyed. St Michael and All Angels Church burned completely out of control and was reduced to an empty shell. The vicarage and church hall were also severely damaged. Two house fires in Ravenscroft Road completed the dramatic scene of flame and smoke so far as habitable property went. Much else was on fire in gardens and backyards - tool sheds, greenhouses, fencing, hen houses, and the like. These were left to be dealt with by householders and fireguards, or to burn themselves out.

Elsewhere in the borough, St John's Vicarage, Eden Park Avenue was damaged by fire - the Revd. W. J. Berry being slightly injured when his garage and car went up in flames. Standard Bank's sports pavilion at Stanhope Grove was another building to be ignited; and a UXB blocked the line at Beckenham Junction station.

Croydon and Purley were swamped by over 8,000 IBs. In South Croydon a mass of houses and other properties on fire overwhelmed the NFS, who were unable to contain the flames. Yet matters were actually worse in West Norwood where 70 NFS units battled with a host of fires that virtually gutted the central shopping area from end to end.

The raid cost the GAF fifteen aircraft from all causes, among which were four brought down by AA guns. It was almost the end of *Steinbock*. What was left of the GAF for operations against Britain would soon be forced to turn its attentions to the south coast invasion ports.

27-28 March: 112 enemy aircraft plotted during a two-hour period. German sources cited Bristol and London as the targets. Bristolians were among the last to know, since no bombs fell on the city. London was under alert for a short spell but no incidents were reported.

April 1944: Some very minor activity over London on several nights in the first half of the month. The last air raid on London to be carried out by manned aircraft was on 18-19 April. Boroughs on the London-Essex borders were the principal hot-spots. The nearest incidents to Bromley appear to have been in the Croydon-Purley area.

Steinbock cost the enemy a minimum of 250 aircraft destroyed, quite possibly over 300. Now peace from aerial attacks descended on the London Region - but only for two months. For then the British capital became the target for the first operational use of the world's first 'cruise missile', the V1 flying bomb.

43) Lych Gate at St Katharine's Church, Knockholt erected as a memorial to the civilians of the village killed by enemy action in the Second World War. Among them was the Revd. Charles Hobley, aged 84, who died from burns when the Rectory was set ablaze, 1am, 22 March 1944. (Lewis Blake)

44) *Holy Trinity Church. Anerley Road (junction with Croydon Road). The church was destroyed on 25 March 1944, in the final raid in which the Bromley area was bombed by manned aircraft. Initially replaced by a church hall, the site is now occupied by housing.*

f Sunday Graphic

45) The Revd. W. J. Berry
(on right in air raid
warden's tunic), Vicar of
St John's Church, Eden
Park. He was slightly
injured when his garage
and car went up in
flames in the raid of
24-25 March 1944.

46) Church of St Michael and All Angels, Ravenscroft Road, Beckenham engulfed by an out-
of-control blaze in the Baby Blitz, 25 March 1944. This was among some sixty
properties burning together in and around Birkbeck Road. (The Late Revd. L. Smith)

Most of the bombardment was concentrated in an eleven-week period, during which some 250 VIs fell in the Bromley area and perhaps another thousand passed overhead, each time causing anxiety and tension for those watching or listening on the ground. The main campaign ended when British-Canadian troops overran the last of the launching sites in France. This did not end the VI threat entirely. From 7 July the enemy began air-launchings from He111s over the North Sea, which continued regularly until January 1945, followed by a period of land-launched robots from Holland in March 1945. The great majority were shot down by AA fire or RAF fighters.

It is beyond the scope of this book to describe, or even mention, each local incident, although every bomb caused massive damage whenever the target was in or near a built-up area. Each had the power and destructive capability of the largest parachute mine, made worse in that they fell by day as well as night, catching people unprotected going about their normal business.

An unusual feature of the first day's bombardment in and around Bromley was the large number of Civil Defence casualties at several separate incidents. The very first incident at 1.30am was at 20 Shawfield Park, Bromley Council Depot and NFS fire station. Denys Spratt, a CD supervisor, was killed nearby, and three NFS men were injured. Half an hour later six CD personnel lost their lives in an ambulance station at the entrance to Willersley Park, Sidcup (Marlborough Park Avenue). At 6am a hit in South Hill Road, Shortlands (junction with Tootswood Road) caused six civilian deaths, including three wardens in an ARP Post (Mr and Mrs R. A. Seath and one other). A Royal Engineers workshop and several army lorries were destroyed here, and there may have been some military casualties.

And then at 8am the blast from a direct hit on 2 Links Road, West Wickham, which was an unoccupied house used by Barwell & Sons for storing furniture, caught heavy rescue workers in a passing lorry. The wrecked vehicle burst into flames and six occupants died, who included war heroes, Frank Burton, OBE and George Wingham, MM. These CD personnel are buried in a mass grave at Beckenham Crematorium close by the mass grave of Beckenham AFS firemen.

Also among targets hit in the first 24 hours was Southborough Lane, Bromley. Here the missile exploded on the grass verge outside No. 412, destroying or badly damaging 25 houses and injuring ten people.

Many local residents went back to the old Blitz routine of spending nights in shelters. In view of continual bombardment for the rest of the summer, it would have been needlessly reckless to remain indoors at night, unless the house was equipped with a Morrison shelter or some other reinforced refuge. Mrs Kennedy in Addington Village recorded in her diary, "Guns firing and shrapnel falling all night and nearly all day... Our roof blasted by a flying bomb in the park, Mother and I sleeping in the Anderson again".

It was different during the day. Life and work and fighting the war had to go on. Cover would be taken only when the rattle of an approaching Doodlebug was heard - usually preceded by warning sirens. The malevolent objects might be watched warily as they crossed the sky, urged on their way by many silent, and un-neighbourly, prayers to 'keep going'. Standing out in the open in this way was rendered less hazardous by the removal of all AA guns from London a few days after the opening shots. No good purpose was served by shooting down the VIs in built-up areas. So the guns went first to the Wealden area of Kent and Sussex and then to the south coast where they proved much more effective against the robots. London's faithful barrage balloons also ceased to grace the capital's skies; they were laid out to produce a dense barrier of cables along the North Downs. Some were just within Orpington's boundary; hence a number of VIs were brought down by balloon cables along the southern edge of what is now part of the London Borough of Bromley.

The district of Penge, covering a mere 800 acres, suffered grievous loss of life and property from 18 Doodlebugs in total. According to the writer's calculations, Penge was close behind Bermondsey, Stepney and Deptford as the worst hit districts in the London Region. The usual practice has been to rank boroughs by number of hits, without making allowance for district size. Hence, larger boroughs south of the Thames, e.g., Croydon, Wandsworth,

48) Tylney Road, Bromley. It was thought to have been blasted in the early tours of 16 June 1944 by the same missile which struck Shawfield Park.

49) West Wickham High Street. Severely blasted more than once during the 'Doodlebug Summer', the most damaging incidents were on 11 July and 12 July.

50) Bickley and Widmore School, Tylney Road. Included here among flying bomb incidents, but the damage could relate to a bombing in the Blitz. Either way, the school was left a sorry mess.

and Lewisham became ranked as worst bombed in that order. At 14.4 missiles to the square mile, Penge was more intensively attacked than the large districts. It also had one of the worst casualty rates: 4.7 killed + 30 injured per missile. Beckenham was also among the badly bombed for its size: 11.7 missiles per square mile. London Region averages were: 2.9 missiles per square mile and casualties of 2.2 killed + 17 injured per missile.

51) Two flying bombs close together in Church Road, Beckenham and by the corner of Albermarle Road and High Street spread devastation over a wide area - afterwards cleared and transformed into an open space of grassland and named Beckenham Green. The picture shows the blast effects in Albemarle Road.

52) A wide view of the destruction in Church Road, Beckenham due to a second direct hit on almost the same spot in the centre of the town, 27 July 1944.

53) *Church Road, Beckenham was obliterated by the V1 hit on 27 July 1944. The road linked Church Hill (the High Street) with St George's Road (now a car park). The break in the pavement in this picture shows where it joined St George's Road, and the footpath through Beckenham Green shows its approximate line. (Lewis Blake)*

The worst incidents in Penge were as follows:

Penge High St 18 June, 3.10am. 11 killed at Nos. 26 & 32. 26 injured. Nos. 26-30 demolished and Nos. 12-70 and 43-109 severely damaged.

Crampton Road 22 June, 11am. Three killed at Nos. 90 and 119, including an 18-year-old army cadet.

Cottingham Road 29 June, 00.20am. Two killed, 31 injured. High Street badly blasted. Fire broke out at Olby's warehouse.

Laurel Grove 29 June, 00.55am. Three killed, 13 injured.

Anerley Town Hall 29 June, 11.10am. Anerley Town Hall, on HAA gun-site at rear. One killed, four injured.

Oak Grove Road 30 June, 11.16am. Four killed, 31 injured.

Trenholme Road 2 July, 9.28am. 13 people killed, 52 injured, 21 houses demolished and 311 damaged.

Palace Square 10 July, 5.58pm. Nine killed, 67 injured; 8 houses destroyed, 200 damaged.

Anerley Road 11 July, 6.10pm. Reportedly a D/H on public shelter. Death toll put as high as 17, with 92 injured. Nine of the victims died at 15 & 66

Anerley Road. Fire broke out in the debris of a bakery.

Penge High St., Junction of Blenheim Road. 21 July. 6.54am. Nine deaths at 3-7 Blenheim Road, including five members of the Carter family. These houses destroyed. 26 injuries. 41 shops and 75 houses severely damaged. 200 shops and houses moderately or slightly damaged. That afternoon the High Street was hit again, with houses destroyed in the vicinity of No. 106.

Wordsworth Road 3 August, 11.20am. Three killed, 42 injured. Three houses destroyed, 112 shops and houses damaged.

Anerley Town Hall 24 August, 7.50pm. At rear on AA gun site (second time hit). 7 killed, 18 injured.

Whatever may be the popular belief about lightning never striking the same spot twice, V1 flying bombs had a pronounced propensity to do exactly that, give or take a few yards. Sometimes multiple hits happened within hours of one another. In retrospect it can be seen that if a V1 fell close to one's home or place of work, the statistical risk of more hits nearby rose significantly. They had got your range! If you could leave, commonsense said 'Go'. Official evacuation schemes were laid on for children, mothers of small children, expectant mothers, and certain other groups. Very large numbers took advantage of going, typically to Wales, the Midlands, and the North. There was nothing like a close encounter with one of the mechanical assailants to convince waverers that prudence was the better part of valour.

Many examples of two or more V1s striking the same spot can be cited from south east London. An outstanding case concerned the centre of Bromley, in London Road on the night of 25-26 June. Two V1s fell on the same stretch of road at 00.50am and 12.40pm. At this distance in time it is difficult to establish how much destruction was owed to the first blast and how much to the second, since the damage merged. A total of 22 shops, flats and houses were destroyed. Park End in particular was severely blasted. 720 shops and houses were damaged as far as the Market Square, also The Beech Tree and The Laurel pubs, the Central Hall (gutted in the Blitz), Christ Church in Highland Road, and the chapel, lodge, and registrar's office of Bromley Cemetery.

Reported casualties were given as eight killed and 67 injured. Seven fatalities occurred at 46-52 Park End and one at 47 London Road. Evidence of this double blast may be seen today in the extensive post-war building in London Road; the Beech Tree pub, for instance, is a post-war re-build of the original.

The old borough of Bromley was the target for 37 flying bombs. Some of those not already mentioned were as follows:

Bickley Road, 18 June, 8pm. Farrants Cottage destroyed. St George's Church and Vicarage severely damaged - the vicar's wife reported injured. St Christopher's School partly demolished. Boughton Hotel in Bickley Park Road badly damaged. A young boarder sheltering in the basement of Bickley

Hall School, 400 yards away, remembered, "the crash of glass was enormous".

Mead Way, Hayes, 23 June, 10.30pm. Four killed, 28 injured. Nos. 52-58 destroyed.

Treewall Gardens, 27 June, 3.45am. Nos. 32-36 destroyed and fire broke out in debris. 440 houses damaged. Four killed at No. 32, including a husband, wife and 14-year-old daughter.

Bickley Station, 30 June, 1.40am. On railway track. Train wrecked and set on fire. Station damaged. 800ft of track uprooted.

Martin's Road, 1 July, 1pm. A direct hit on terraced cottages close to Shortlands station extended Blitz destruction caused by a one ton bomb in 1941, with the consequence that today the greater part of the road is blocks of flats where Victorian cottages once stood. Damage embraced all shops in Shortlands, the Valley School, the Congregational Church, Shortlands Tavern, Whitehall Laundry (set on fire in the Blitz), and the station itself.

Wendover Road, 10 July. Five persons killed at Nos. 28 and 32.

Crown Lane, 15 July, 1.56pm. Mid-air explosion. Probably due to an RAF interception. One person killed at No. 101.

Freelands Road, 22 July, 2.05am. Nursery gardens hit. Offices and greenhouses destroyed. Blast damage extended to Market Square and Bromley High Street.

Hayes Lane, 1 August. Bromley County School For Boys. Thought to have been in the grounds. School and nearby properties extensively damaged.

Judging by the distribution of incidents between Bromley and Ladywell, at least one launch ramp in France seemed to be nicely, if fortuitously, aligned with the A21 Hastings Road along this length. The mean track, apparently on a 320-330° bearing, originated in the Abbeville area. Twenty or more V1s came down within 200-300 yards either side of the road, among them the double-incident in London Road. A cluster of seven or eight hits occurred around Southend Village/ Southend Lane; and another cluster of five or six just south and SE of Rushey Green, Catford, plus a direct hit on Lewisham Hospital.

The writer remembers seeing an example of a V1 'tracking' the A21 when standing one evening at the top of Beckenham Hill Road. Presumably we were under air raid alert, but during daylight hours this seldom made us take cover unless directly threatened. The unmistakable rasping rattle of an approaching Buzz Bomb caused me to turn towards the sound - and there was the little black monster racing along parallel with Bromley Road at maybe 1,000 feet, crossing Southend Village in full view and hurtling towards Bellingham and Catford. Why it stuck in the mind was the unusual sight of a fighter - RAF Typhoon - giving chase in disregard of instructions not to intercept over London. Disappointingly, it showed no sign of gaining on the intruder. Both machines raced on, lost to view, and no more was heard of either from where the present writer stood.

The former borough of Beckenham was particularly hard hit in the centre of the town and in most surrounding districts. Whatever one may read in official and semi-official accounts about the V1's inaccuracy, the fact remains that the prevalence of bunched hits showed potential consistency of aim which, if the *Luftwaffe* had had access to reliable information about falls, could have been used to score hits on or near valuable military and economic targets.

The grass of Beckenham Green between Beckenham High Street, Albemarle Road and St George's Street marks the site of devastation caused by an example of a double-attack. The first missile at 3am on 3 July smashed into Albemarle Road, killing three people at No. 7 and injuring 30. Eleven shops in Albemarle Road and 38 in Church Hill were severely damaged; also St George's Church, the church hall (used as a British Restaurant - cheap, hot meals designed for the working population), the Railway Hotel, Beckenham Public Hall, etc.

The second missile fell at 5.40pm, 27 July and was a direct hit on 5 Church Road. Three lives were lost at Nos. 7-8. Twenty five people were injured and eight houses and a bakery destroyed. Damage encompassed 53 houses, 38 shops, the Railway Hotel, four banks, St George's parish church (all stained glass windows blown out), Beckenham fire station, and St George's School. Church Road eventually disappeared from the map to become part of the grassed area. Church Hill is now usually treated as part of the High Street.

Whether the Germans intended to strike a double blow at Elmers End industry on 18 July we shall probably never find out. We know that they succeeded more than they could have imagined. At 8am the explosion in Croydon Road started a serious fire at Surridges Patents Ltd., which was fought by nine NFS crews. Other factories damaged included Muirhead's, H. Flack Ltd., and Marsh Motors. A member of the Home Guard was reported killed in the roadway.

Then at 8.30pm a direct hit on Elmers End bus garage killed 18 people, including 11 London Transport staff, a rescue worker, and a woman in a nearby air raid shelter. About 50 others sustained serious injuries. The garage was totally wrecked by the blast and a raging inferno that followed it. Parked close together, buses burst into flames in rapid succession. Tyres ignited at once and sump casings burned fiercely like incendiary bombs because of their magnesium content. 38 double-deckers and Green Line coaches became complete write-offs, burned down to the chassis.

NFS firemen and rescue workers found people trapped under the debris of the canteen and offices and in grave danger of being burned alive. Only their courage and sheer guts prevented a much greater disaster, for the risks they faced were not just from scorching flames, burning embers, choking smoke, and falling debris - underneath the garage floor 500 gallons of petrol, 8,500 gallons of Diesel fuel, and fifty cases of Home Guard hand grenades, small arms ammunition, mortars, etc., threatened to go up in a gigantic fireball which might have incinerated everyone....

SE London's second worst VI incident (Lewisham Clock Tower was the worst) wiped out 44 lives in Beckenham Road at 1pm, 2 August. The missile swooped down on Richards' dining rooms at No. 199 when it was crowded with lunchtime customers, who stood no chance. The dead included Albert Richards (restaurant owner), Sidney Hancock (fishmonger at No. 195), the wife and daughter of Philip Rust (tailor), and Edwin Finch (grocer at No. 197). The author's next-door neighbour in Catford was among the diners to lose their lives. Several victims died in Beckenham Hospital.

The blast destroyed 14 shops and 12 houses; smashed the Prince Arthur pub (re-built as The Clock House); severely damaged a dance hall, 17 shops and 42 houses; slightly damaged 18 shops and 124 houses; and caused four fires to break out in debris and another in the roof of a wrecked shop. Mounds of masonry blocked this main road between Penge and Beckenham for many hours. One way and another the whole area was so badly blitzed in the war that wholesale re-development took place afterwards between Clock House station and the railway bridge, which now carries the Croydon TramLink.

Other VI blasts in the old borough of Beckenham included the following:

Westfield Road 23 June, 8am. Four killed at Nos. 13 and 22. Six NFS pumps in attendance. Ten houses destroyed. Shops at 202-234 Croydon Road damaged.

Queen's Road 26 June, 1am. Nos. 38-50 and 37-49 wrecked. Fires broke out in the ruins of Nos. 41-43. 127 houses damaged.

West Wickham High St. 28 June, 5.30pm. Homes destroyed, fires in debris. 15 shops badly damaged.

Rectory Road 28 June, 5.40pm. Extensive damage to the ABC Regal cinema and the shopping centre.

Shortlands Road, 28 June, 8pm. Four killed (one at No. 75). Two large detached houses demolished.

King's Hall Road 3 July. Three died.

West Wickham High St. 11 July, 5.50pm. Exploded in the roadway. One person killed, 20 injured. Bus and cars destroyed by fire and blast. Many shops badly damaged.

The Grove, West Wickham (off the High Street), 12 July, 8.55am. Second attack within hours. One killed, 26 injured. NFS fireman reported with head injury from a splinter of the bomb. No. 23 The Grove destroyed, fire broke out in the ruins. 300 shops and houses now damaged in and around this end of the High Street.

j/o Church & Kingswood Roads, Shortlands, 22 July, 1am. Severe damage to St Mary's Parish Church and church hall (in use as a Rest Centre), the Vicarage, and an ARP Post.

Bramerton Road 27 July, 1.40am. Five deaths. Five houses destroyed, 600 damaged. (Hit again on 2 August at 8.20am)

j/o St Mary's Avenue & Church Road, Shortlands, 27 July, 3.30pm.
St Mary's Church badly damaged again and required demolition. Re-built
after the war. Also 25 houses severely damaged.
Druids Way/ Kingswood Avenue, Shortlands, 3 August, 10.55am. One
person killed, 16 injured. Five houses destroyed, 152 damaged.

Most people probably know from descriptions of the weather around D-
Day, 6 June 1944, just how unsettled and unreliable conditions were on many
dates in that summer. But rain and low cloud cover did not impede the robot
bombs in the slightest. On the other hand, they made the task of the
defenders more difficult and added to the strain on the general population
through their not being able to judge by sound alone the degree of danger
posed by a passing robot.

On the opening night of the bombardment, 10/10th multi-layered cloud
covered south east England, with widespread rain and drizzle and the cloud
base down to 1,000ft in places. The next 24 hours were little better: 10/10th
cloud at 3,000-4,000ft; clear patches over London after midnight; and a
20mph NW wind. A few days later on 23 June there was 10/10th cloud base
at 800ft until 10am; 9/10th cover at 1,500ft at 1pm; 6/10th cloud at 3,000ft
at 4pm; almost clear sky after 10pm. 2 July was a particularly unpleasant day:
7/10th cloud and prolonged rainy periods. "Horrible day", Mrs Kennedy
confided in her diary. "Rain and flying bombs all day." On the 3rd thundery
conditions developed and because of the risk of lightning, barrage balloons
on the North Downs were grounded from 9.20am until 5.10pm.

The conditions on 2-3 July seemed to contribute to a worse performance by
the defences in daylight than at night. Of 45 missiles launched in daylight, 5
crashed at sea, just 7 were destroyed by AA fire or balloons, and none by the
RAF. 31 crashed on London (69% of launchings). In the hours of darkness, 68
missiles were launched - 5 crashed at sea, 14 were brought down by AA fire,
16 by the RAF, and 3 by balloons. 28 reached London (41% of launchings).

The weather definitely made a difference. In the Battle of Britain and the
Blitz, old-fashioned British summer conditions favoured the defenders.
Against flying bombs they helped the enemy.

A further complication for the defenders began to emerge in July. Although
not realised as such by the British for a few days, the first air-launched V1s
from He111s over the North Sea were fired on the night of 7 July. These
approached London from the east and therefore outflanked the elaborate
'Diver' defences to the south of London. For just three or four nights
between 11-14 July the Heinkels concentrated on Portsmouth and
Southampton rather than London, with wildly inaccurate results.

Summary of selected incidents elsewhere in the Bromley area

Chelsfield Lane, 19 June, 9pm. Elderly man and wife killed in their cottage 'Lillys'. Thought to have been a V1 brought down by balloon.

21 Mottingham Road, George Hyde's motor works, 21 June, 4.20am D/H. Four killed, ten injured. Two-thirds of works destroyed by fire and blast. 40 cars burnt out. 253 houses damaged.

Biggin Hill airfield, 23 June, 8.50am. D/H on North Camp. NFS pumps rushed to scene where fires and blast severely damaged the officers mess and quarters, transport and clothing stores, and the Salvation Army canteen.

21 Mottingham Road, 26 June, 2.45am. Second D/H on George Hyde's motor works which finished off the premises. All contents destroyed by fire and blast. Eltham College and the shopping area damaged.

Bombers Lane, Biggin Hill, 26-27 June, 11.45pm. Two cottages and a balloon destroyed. Suggests V1 was brought down by balloon cable.

Salt Box Hill, Biggin Hill, 26-27 June, 4.30am. Large fire at RAF premises. 11 NFS pumps sent to scene.

St Hugh's College, Chislehurst Road, 26-27 June, 5.40am. College half demolished. Was in use by publishers, Hodder & Stoughton. Nelson's motor works badly damaged. Northfield Nursing Home and Bird-In-Hand pub slightly damaged.

Towncourt Crescent, Petts Wood, 26-27 June, 6.25pm. Nos. 36-46 severely damaged; 320 houses slightly damaged. 37 persons injured.

Berrys Green, 28-29 June, 11pm. Homeleigh Farm damaged. 200ft of wire and a dry battery indicated the V1 was equipped with W/T which signalled range back to France.

Old Tye Avenue, Biggin Hill, 28-29 June, 10.46am. V1 brought down by balloon cable. 15 injured. (see below)

Gordon King was a 15-year-old delivering bread in Old Tye Avenue when the Doodlebug struck a balloon cable and came veering towards him. He and his colleague, Stan Matthews, jumped under the bread van, "...knowing we were going to die. Stan said to me 'this one's ours, boy' and we waited for the impact". Gordon held his head as a large section of the V1 embedded itself in the vehicle. After a few moments, he and Stan climbed out to a scene of chaos. A man was walking towards them carrying a baby. "I don't know where he came from, but he was bleeding profusely and the baby was covered in blood as well. He handed the baby to me and then just collapsed."

In shock, Gordon sprinted 200 yards to an ARP Post where he handed the baby to a warden. Sixty years later and a grandfather, Gordon recalled in the local *News Shopper*, "The baby can't have been more than a few months old and to this day I do not know what happened to it or whether it was a boy or a girl".

Weald House, Crockham Hill (Westerham), 30 June. V1 shot down by the RAF. Exploded directly on Weald House, which was in use as a nursery for infants evacuated from London. 22 infants and six nurses lost their lives in the disaster.

Lillys Wood, Chelsfield, 21 July, 2.32pm. V1 brought down by balloon cable.

Green Lane, Chislehurst, 21 July, 7.17pm. Four killed at No. 145; 11 injured. Six houses destroyed, 39 severely damaged.

Lakes Road, Keston, 24 July, 6.25pm. Five killed, including an ARP warden, 30 injured. 11 houses destroyed. 150 damaged as far as Commonside, Fox Lane, Fishponds Road, Croydon Road, etc. 12 NFS pumps called to deal with fires and help in rescue work. The blast overturned beehives in one garden, and enraged insects repeatedly stung a man lying unconscious on the ground. A policeman, though also repeatedly stung, rescued the victim, but fell seriously ill for some weeks. The rescued casualty died later from his injuries and the effects of 130 bee stings. Three NFS men also fell ill due to multiple bee stings.

Princes Avenue, Petts Wood, 27 July, 5.55pm. 30 injured. 480 houses damaged.

Willow Grove, Chislehurst, 29 July, 2.15pm. 5 deaths, 20 injuries. Four homes destroyed. Two schools, two churches, 66 shops, and 368 houses damaged.

The campaign attained its maximum effect on 3 August with 97 missiles coming to ground in the London Region, all apparently air-launched over the sea between the latitudes of Ostend and Rotterdam. The enemy took full advantage of 10/10th cloud cover as low as 300ft throughout the day, which severely restricted RAF operations. Londoners wondered, with good cause, how much longer this sort of thing could go on before all their homes were in ruins. What they experienced on this date was, in fact, a kind of one-off gesture of defiance by the *Luftwaffe* - a warning that the V1 attacks would not end with the capture of the fixed sites in France. Incidents dropped off sharply within a day or two, all the same. The steady capture of sites in the Pas de Calais by Canadian troops, rapid improvement in the success rate of the Diver defences, and the enemy's inability to maintain air-launchings at a high level were the main factors in this welcome turn of events.

The biggest social challenge of the long bombardment was its enormous legacy of destroyed and uninhabitable homes in the London Region, compounded by later V2 rocket attacks. Over one million homes needed urgent repairs before winter set in, and many thousands of experienced workers in the building trades came to the London area from across the UK to assist in the mammoth task. Eventually 40 per cent of the nation's total building work force was engaged in the undertaking. One might say it was only right and proper that the rest of the country, which had mercifully escaped the Buzz Bomb ordeal, should lend this support. It was no mean sacrifice, nevertheless, for middle-aged men to be separated by long distances and for long periods from their families, living in austerity hostels and private digs in the depths of winter among strangers, sharing the same dangers from V2 rockets and V1s.

Bromley's tally of missiles on 3 August (NB. All dates are 24 hour periods from 6am to 6am) was at least fifteen. Two have been noted already under district headings. Among others were Biggin Hill (King's Road), Sidcup Station (severely damaged, along with numerous shops and houses), RAF Biggin Hill (runway damaged), High Street, Downe (two incidents - one a mid-air explosion after RAF interception, the other injuring nine people in the vicinity of High Elms Road), Felstead Road, Orpington (22 injured), Blake's Recreation Ground, West Wickham (155 shops and houses damaged), and Sundridge Avenue, Bromley (70 houses damaged).

The intensity of the day's operations was reflected in the expenditure of AA ammunition, namely, 24,592 heavy rounds and 12,460 Bofors and Hispano rounds by guns all round the coast from the Thames Estuary to Newhaven. The stretch between Littlestone and Rye had the busiest time, where 4,615 90mm rounds fired by American batteries were included in the HAA total. Altogether, AA fire shot down 46 robots, barrage balloons did unusually well, bagging 18 (Was this because some missiles flew along the barrage instead of across it?), but due to bad weather the RAF tally was only seven.

By the end of August, with the last sites in France firing off all their stocks before being over-run, the Diver defences were thoroughly in control of the campaign. 99 launchings in the Pas de Calais were detected on 28 August. RAF fighters shot down 13 over the Channel, AA guns shot down 45 off the coast and 26 more as they crossed it. This left only 15. RAF fighters shot down nine of these overland, leaving six only for the balloon barrage, which brought down two. Only four reached London; none cut-out and fell while crossing the Bromley area.

For Bromley the main summer bombardment ended on the morning of 31 August with the V1 which plunged into the playing fields of Beckenham County School for Boys. This coincided with the last hits elsewhere in SE London, at Woolwich Arsenal, Falconwood Station, and Maryon Wilson Park, Charlton. Between them they took one life and injured 29. The last firings from France occurred next day: just five shots, none of which reached London.

Mrs Kennedy wrote in her diary on 1 September, "Slept indoors again for the first time since 17 June". Which said it all.

54) Elmer's End bus garage photographed when newly built in 1929.

55) A direct hit on Elmers End Bus Garage, 18 July 1944, produced a fierce conflagration which left the garage a charred and twisted shell containing the burnt remains of 38 buses and coaches fused together in a single, molten mass. 18 people lost their lives in this disaster, including eleven London Transport staff.

56) Beckenham Road, Beckenham, April 1903, looking west towards the future site of Richards' Café, on the left.

57) One of the worst V1 incidents of all occurred here in Beckenham Road, just yards from Clock House station, when a crowded café (Richards') sustained a direct hit, on 2 August 1944. 44 people died under tons of rubble. The destruction, seen here, stretched to the railway bridge, which now carries the Croydon Tramway.

58) *The same scene today (2005) The Prince Arthur pub was re-built as The Clock House (centre of picture). (Lewis Blake)*

59) *Hyde's Motor Works Mottingham c.1930. George Hyde's motor works suffered two direct hits by flying bombs in June 1944, which destroyed the plant completely and led to many casualties. (F.J.Mott)*

60) On the far corner in Mottingham Road a petrol station stands on the site of the old motor works. (Lewis Blake)

61) Lakes Road, Keston. Houses that replaced cottages destroyed on the evening of 24 July 1944. Among several fatalities was an injured victim stung to death by enraged bees whose hives had been overturned by the blast. (Lewis Blake)

CHAPTER 13

Bolts from the Blue

"A long shot, Watson, a very long shot!"
(The Memoirs of Sherlock Holmes)

Such was Hitler's obsession with the idea of an eleventh hour reign of vengeance on the British capital as a desperate way of altering the course of the war that even the virtual eclipse of the V1 offensive failed to end London's mortal peril from his next retaliatory secret weapon - the V2 rocket. What now awaited the civilian population opened a new, dark chapter in remote, push-button warfare.

There was no effective method available in 1944 for warning the public of a V2's approach or for destroying it in flight. With its journey from firing pad in Holland to target taking rather less than five minutes and having a terminal velocity of 2,500-2,700mph, the V2 was immune to conventional counter-measures. The missile exploded before those near heard its approach. As the Metropolitan Police historian put it, "If you heard it, you were all right; if you didn't, you might not be".

The irony was that absence of warnings, of hostile aircraft, and of all the noisy trappings of previous bombardments took away the immediate fear, as well as the pressing need to be continually spending hours in shelters. There was so little of practical value that civilians could do about Hitler's rockets that most went on with their ordinary lives without worrying unduly. The time to worry, to feel terror, was when one dropped close by; but then it was too late to worry. Till then, it was best to carry on, keep one's fingers crossed, and think about something else.

Provided the loud explosions were not too frequent and one was spared personal involvement in a particular incident, fatalism seems to have been the governing feeling - not so as to interfere with one's daily tasks and duties, nor with recreations and amusements; just a kind of surrealist, detached fatalism which simply ignored this terrible backdrop to life's routine.

Had the bombardment reached the intensity planned by the enemy, matters would have turned out very differently. Compulsory evacuation from London for all those whose presence was not essential appears to have been the government's contingency plan in the event of saturation attack. Plans included 87 secret dispersal routes. For example, Beckenham refugees would have assembled at the ABC Regal cinema for a fast despatch by bus to the Sevenoaks area. Another assembly point was the old King's Hall in Penge.

The arrival of a V2 was perceived over a wider area than that travelled by the sound of the explosion. A loud double-report was often heard for many miles around. This led to a good deal of speculation and many letters to the authorities in the weeks preceding official admission that England was under long-range rocket (LRR) attack. In general terms, a double-report would be heard in places which the missile had passed over before ground impact. One report was the sharp thunderclap of the sonic boom created by the missile's supersonic flight through the lower atmosphere. No one knew about sonic booms at that time, so these great aerial crashes were a considerable mystery; even scientists were not sure how to explain them.

A shuddering explosion followed the sonic boom almost instantly or after a lapse of a second or two, depending on where one was in relation to the POI (Point Of Impact). At 'ground-zero' the blast wave drowned out everything. If the V2 fell short of where one was located, the explosion would be heard followed by heavy rumbling of atmospheric disturbance. No sonic boom occurred at ground level in these circumstances. Within a few hundred yards of a fall the massive explosion might be followed by eerie and unnerving roaring noises rushing skywards in a kind of vertical acoustic vortex. These were the sounds of the rocket's supersonic descent reaching ground level in reverse time order.

Visual perceptions were fairly rare. Most sightings occurred in the early sunrise in the eastern sky, and they usually took the form of a vapour and smoke trail rising at a prodigious rate to a tremendous height. If the low-angled sunlight caught the rocket's flaming trail, a vivid light was seen ascending like "frozen lightning, almost too bright to look at", as one witness described it. Soon the vapour trail became wavy and faded, and the weapon's progress was lost to view. Two minutes later might be heard a double-report or a single explosion with thunder-like rumbling - faintly in the far distance, or too close for comfort.

Sightings were not usually deliberately sought out. There was too much else to do and think about than to get up at the crack of dawn in the hope of spotting the harbinger of one's own demise! A typical visual glimpse was that experienced by Miss Margaret Cox, a teacher at Alexandra's Infants School in Beckenham, when one morning she was returning by train to her home in Dulwich after a night's social work in Chislehurst Caves. She happened to be looking out of the window of her compartment, her back to the engine while the train was standing at Penge East station, when she noticed a white column of smoke or vapour climbing rapidly into the sky far away beyond the skyline of Shooters Hill. She wondered idly whether what she was seeing was "one of those rockets coming over that people were talking about..."

Her next thought was to wish the train would get going into Sydenham tunnel before the wretched thing, whatever it was, fell on them. Her wish was granted, so she never heard what happened next. How typical, too, was the scant interest shown by others in her story. Half a century later Margaret Cox was still wondering whether what she had seen as a young teacher had actually been a V2 rocket, for no one she talked to had the slightest idea.

A glimpse of a rocket in the final stage of its trajectory might take the form of a pencil-like object drawing an oily, brown line across the sky at phenomenal speed. If you missed this rare and fleeting moment, you might still see broken streaks of oily brown smoke hanging in the sky for twenty or thirty seconds after a missile had plunged to earth. At night, a descending missile could be seen like a red-hot poker flashing past; not as fast or as fleeting as a shooting star, yet only in view for maybe three or four seconds. It might also appear as a bright light in this way. Any V2 which came down enveloped in flames offered an altogether more dramatic picture; more so if it exploded in mid-air, as some did.

The V2 bombardment opened with two shots on Chiswick and Parndon Woods, Epping within moments of each other in the late afternoon of 8 September 1944. If these were ranging shots, then it was a remarkable piece of marksmanship - straddling the target (central London) from 200 miles away at first attempt. All that the German artillery units now needed was reliable information on where their shots went in order to refine their aim for the greatest effect. This, the British were determined to deny them, in the first instance by declining even to admit for several weeks that any rockets had fallen on the country. Then by the exercise of strict censorship, combined with misleading information fed to German intelligence by 'turned' German agents controlled from London.

Odd to think that while people suffering the attacks were kept in the dark - this official silence added to the surrealist atmosphere pervading London in the autumn of 1944 - those responsible for the attacks were receiving regular, albeit misleading, reports on the fall of shots. Lots of Londoners reading a *Daily Express* report headed WHERE DO MY V2s GO? HITLER IS ASKING, might well have thought, "Well, if Hitler ever finds out, perhaps he'll tell us!"

The first rocket in the Bromley area came down at Field Crouch Farm, Crockenhill at 9.07am, 11 September. It was the fourth V2 to land so far. No damage or casualties resulted. Almost exactly 24 hours later, rocket No. 8 on England exploded among trees at Layhams Farm, Keston, about 1 1/2 miles from Biggin Hill airfield. Again no damage or casualties was reported. Several days passed, then rocket No. 21 exploded on open ground at Cudham. V2 fragments found two miles to the east near Knockholt Pound suggested the missile had disintegrated in mid-air, with the warhead flying on to Cudham. Once more there were no casualties.

These explosions thundered and reverberated for miles around, across the suburbs and among the folds and valleys of the North Downs, to the great mystification of the populace. Other unexplained loud bangs and crashes had come from the direction of London. Yet the Bromley area had been lucky so far: a hat-trick of harmless misses to the south, plus three serious incidents within audible distance in Woolwich, Brockley, and Lambeth.

How long would Bromley's luck hold out? Several weeks more, all thanks to Operation Market Garden, which obliged German V2 batteries to abandon The Hague and Walcheren Island for fear of being cut off. The Arnhem operation wasn't a bridge too far for London. It saved hundreds of civilian lives in the end by interrupting the build-up of rocket attacks just as German artillery units were settling in to the job. Meanwhile, they targeted East Anglia, since it was within range of their new positions. The ultimate failure of Arnhem, however, permitted the rocket batteries to return to The Hague area and resume their attacks on London.

It was Crockenhill again where the first V2 in the Bromley area fell in the resumed bombardment (31 October 1944). Same results, too: no casualties, no damage to buildings, just a large hole in a field. During November, targets included Davenport Road, Sidcup (26 injured, on the 6th), Bushey Avenue/Towncourt Lane, Petts Wood (two killed, 25 injured on the 14th), Malvern Road, Orpington (24 injured, on the 21st), airburst over Chislehurst/Sidcup border, east of Cookham Road (on 25th), and Lamorbey Park Hotel, Sidcup (in grounds, six injured, on 27th).

Germany lost patience waiting for some admission from Britain concerning the attacks and on 8 November broadcast to the world that Churchill was deliberately concealing the truth from his people. For good measure the announcement included examples of places allegedly hit. As these were a mish-mash of half-fact, half-fiction passed out by British-controlled agents, they came as no surprise to military intelligence in London.

Raymond Wattenbach, whose boyhood recollections have been quoted previously, was in the dormitory at Bickley Hall School, standing with his back to the window, when he saw a light reflected in a wardrobe mirror descending quite slowly until disappearing from view. The time was just after 9.15pm on Sunday, 19 November 1944. Moments later a massive explosion shook the school to its foundations... Just half-a-mile to the south, the 219th V2 rocket to strike England had come down on the forecourt of The Crooked Billet pub in Southborough Lane with disastrous consequences. The entire four-storey building was collapsed in a huge heap on the lip of a crater 30ft wide by 15ft deep, and houses lay in ruins or badly damaged over a 300 yard radius.

The light Raymond Wattenbach saw reflected in a mirror was probably made by the V2's hot exhaust. Its apparent slow descent would have been due to the high angle of a V2 falling so close. Had the light seemed almost motionless but growing brighter, like the headlights of a car on a head-on collision course with one's own, young Raymond and the other boy boarders may not have lived to tell the tale.

At the scene of devastation, four heavy rescue teams and scores of NFS personnel laboured under floodlights through the hours of darkness and throughout the next day recovering bodies and rescuing survivors. Indefatigable volunteers of the WVS ran a mobile canteen on the site to keep the rescuers supplied with hot drinks and snacks, and they operated an enquiry desk to answer the worries of anxious relatives and friends of missing persons. A mobile FAP treated the slightly injured on the spot, while ambulances ferried more serious cases to Bromley and Farnborough hospitals. Mortuary vans also came and went at intervals.

Recovery of the last bodies called for the complete clearance of the site. The tally stood then at 23 killed, 65 seriously injured, and 34 treated for minor injuries, making this the worst incident of the war for casualties in the old Bromley Borough.

Ray Holledge, then a RAF flying instructor at Cranwell, had been celebrating his mother's 57th birthday in the saloon bar with family and friends a moment before the rocket struck. He was saying good night before leaving to keep a date at Bromley Country Club and had actually reached the front corner entrance when called back to pick up his gloves. Just then the rocket exploded on the very spot where he would otherwise have been. Ray writes, "My mother was killed and everyone else in our party was badly injured. I was later told that friends of ours, Les and Ada Draper, pulled me out of the rubble and by so doing probably saved my life, as there was a subsequent further collapse of the structure."

Peter Whitlock, a 14-year-old schoolboy, with his mother, older brother and younger sister were in their cottage adjacent to the pub. Peter's brother died in the blast, and he, his mother and his sister were seriously injured. Peter and Ray finished up in adjacent beds of Stanley Ward in Bromley Hospital, and Ray recalls, "My injuries were largely to my head, whereas young Peter's legs were badly injured and in consequence he suffered a lot of pain. I tried to console him, especially during the long nights when neither of us could sleep..."

If it's ever possible for tragic stories such as this to have a happy sequel, then the amazing re-union of Peter and Ray 51 years later in 1995 could perhaps qualify. It happened that when Ray and his wife, 'Mick', celebrated their Golden Wedding anniversary, the News Shopper reported the occasion, which Peter spotted. They had not been in touch for half-a-century, but Peter contacted Ray and they arranged a joyful re-union at the re-built Crooked Billet. Ray was not sure how he would recognise the boy he once knew. However, his doubts were resolved when "a gentleman of mature years limped over and threw his arms around me". Since then they regularly dine there each 19 November and, in Ray's words, "remain the firmest of friends".

Given the preoccupation with the much greater threat posed by Hitler's V2 rockets, which were claiming the lives of hundreds of Londoners in some weeks, it is not surprising that some people lost sight of the fact that the capital was still being targeted by air-launched flying bombs. They would have been much more conscious of the dual nature of the enemy's attentions were it not for the fact that AA guns and RAF fighters destroyed the vast majority of VIs which made landfall. General Sir Frederick Pile wrote that ack-ack results were so good that Londoners thought the VI campaign was over in November.

At least the sirens warned of a VI's approach. In October they sounded almost every day, sometimes twice or more in one day. Of the 1,012 Buzz Bombs detected by the defences between early-September 1944 and mid-January 1945, only 66 reached the London Region. Locally, these included in October two incidents in Downe - at Hengrove Hill and Farthing Street - and one at Sidcup. Possibly the worst incident of the autumn-winter VI campaign occurred at Purley at dawn on 31 October, with a direct hit on St Marie Hotel which killed 19 and injured 30.

On this date nine missiles were plotted. Eight made landfall between Southwold and Shoeburyness at 1,000-3,000ft. The RAF shot down two. AA fire shot down three for the expenditure of 976 shells - phenomenally effective fire, made possible by the introduction of the proximity fuse in the summer. Of the trio left, two came down in open countryside and the sole survivor traversed south London before diving on the St Marie Hotel.

January 1945 witnessed two serious flying bomb incidents in the Bromley area. In the first, at 10.45pm on the 5th, another part of central Beckenham was laid waste by this weapon. Falling behind the High Street in Fairfield Road, the bomb destroyed 20 houses and severely damaged 35 more, as well as Christ Church. Nearly 200 shops and houses suffered moderate damage. 13 residents perished in the blast - at 24 Fairfield Road, 40-42 and 151 Burnhill Road, and 1-5 Lea Road - and 32 were injured. To this day the large car park behind the High Street by Christ Church marks the extent of the destruction.

Between 1.42am and 2.14am of the 14th, the defences plotted 13 robot bombs make landfall. Four were shot down by AA guns, and HM drifter *Eadwire* in the Thames Estuary claimed another. Six fell in London, including one on farmland in Keston (Layhams Road/North Pole Lane) and another in Court Road, Orpington which claimed eight lives at Nos. 100-106, destroyed six houses and damaged 400, plus 40 shops, the Commodore Cinema, and J4 sub-divisional fire station at 250 High Street. Both incidents occurred at about 2am.

10/10th cloud at 1,300ft had hindered the defences in this attack, though the VIs flew too low in any event for AA engagement. AA Command called it a "concentrated and well-aimed attack... the launching area was rather more south than usual". It transpired that 14 January 1945 was the last date on which air-launched VIs flew against England. In March, however, a series of land-based launchings of a longer-range VI took place from the vicinity of The Hague, as described later.

63) An impression of some of the damage in Southborough Lane due to the V2 rocket at The Crooked Billet pub. This was Bromley's worst wartime incident for casualties - 23 lives lost and 99 injured, Sunday evening, 19 November 1944.

Returning to the rocket attacks, the main incident locally in December occurred at Jevington Way, Mottingham on the 15th when seven persons were killed at Nos. 41-51 and 57 were injured. Alsatian search dogs successfully located several bodies in the densely packed wreckage. In January 1945, rocket No.427 landed on the Midland Bank Sportsground, Lennard Road, Beckenham on the 2nd, injuring 14, damaging the pavilion, New Beckenham station, and nearby houses. Others fell at Sundridge Avenue/ Logshill Road, Bromley; Addington Golf Course; Brooklands Avenue, Sidcup (three killed, 22 injured); King's Hall Road, Beckenham (Cypher sportsground), 20 injured; and Garden Road, Bromley (one killed, six injured; 45 shops and houses and Sundridge Park Hotel damaged)

64) The Crooked Billet as rebuilt c.1965.

65) A section of the damage in West Common Road, Hayes following a direct hit by a V2 rocket on Grandfield's nurseries, 9 February 1945. James Grandfield and his son were killed in the blast.

66) St John's Church, Eden Park may look in sound condition in this picture. In fact, it was seriously damaged structurally and required to be shored up and largely re-built. The Church hall has virtually collapsed, with just a section left tottering - the work of a V2 rocket on nearby open ground, 21 February 1945. (Mr Stirling, St John's Church)

During February, V2 incidents included the following:

St Mary Cray, 6th., 9.48am. Star Lane, in cemetery.
Chislehurst, 8th., 3.04am. Scadbury Park. Queen Mary Hospital damaged. No casualties reported. (Rocket 696)
Sidcup, 8th., 5.40pm. Berwick Crescent. Exploded in front gardens of Nos. 8-10. Seven killed, 110 injured. 12 houses demolished.
Hayes, 9th., 5.30pm. Grandfield's Nurseries, West Common Road. Four killed, 70 injured. Fatalities included James Grandfield, 62, owner of the nurseries, and his son Stanley, 34. Two shops and five houses destroyed. Hayes Parish Church, Hayes Village Hall, the church hall, The George pub and 13 shops damaged in Hayes Old Village. 290 houses damaged over a wide area. (Rocket 710)
Chislehurst, 9th., 9.30pm. Walden Avenue, on allotments. Two killed, 68 injured. Eight houses destroyed. 340 houses, six shops, the Baptist Church, and the White Horse Inn damaged. (Rocket 712)
Bromley, 11th., 1.36pm. Sundridge Ave. Sundridge Park Hotel damaged for the second time by a V2. (Rocket 730)
Chislehurst, 14th., 2.40pm. Kemnal Road. 'Foxbury', in use as a rest hospital for ATS of No. 4 London Division. No civilian casualties reported. Military casualties not known. (Rocket 765)
Sidcup, 21st., 9.22am. Bunker's Hill. Five injured. (Rocket 839)
Beckenham, 21st., 11.21am. Eden Park Avenue, on open ground by St John's Church. 26 injured, including the Vicar, the Revd. W. J. Berry, who was also hurt in an air raid eleven months earlier. (Rocket 840)

67) After the main flying bomb campaign ended in 1944, only a relatively small handful of the air-launched variety reached the London area. It was central Beckenham's great misfortune to be target of one of them on 5 January 1945. Here behind the High Street in Fairfield, Burnhill and Lea Roads thirteen residents lost their lives. (Bromley Libraries)

As we have seen, public disclosure of V2 incidents was strictly censored while the bombardment continued. In connection with the St John's Church blast, all the *Beckenham Journal* could admit was "a bomb incident in a Southern town recently..."

> "... two Jersey cows and one hen met an untimely end. Several people were treated for cuts at first aid posts and five were taken to hospital... The bomb landed in a field behind a modern Church of England church. The building was badly damaged, the church hall was smashed and the vicarage suffered damage to the roof, ceilings and back windows.... The vicar's young wife said, 'I was in the kitchen on the side nearest the bomb. My 15-month-old baby, Mary, was in her pram by a wall where I always put her, because of the absence of glass. She was asleep and never even woke up. The wall above her pram was horribly cracked... My husband was in his study and was a little cut by glass.'

"Large pieces of the missile heaped on the ground proved very exciting for crowds of school children who hindered policemen and other officials in their work." An old familiar refrain! (Reproduced by permission of Kentish Times Newspapers).

(NB. Rocket numbers refer to a Home Office list, which shows a total of 1,115 incidents on English soil and inshore waters. A second official list shows 1,083 incidents, which omits some inshore reports).

Enemy artillery batteries launched a record 244 successful shots against England in February, and the proportion reaching the London Region showed an upward trend (40% against 34% in December). An average of 8.7 a day was the highest for any single month, marginally higher than March - the final month of the campaign. Fifteen fell in open water close to the shore. A good many mis-fired at launch or came down in the North Sea. These, of course, were not included in the British lists.

Essex and east/NE districts of London continued to receive the major share of falls. The range of shots tended to shorten in an ENE direction, following the direction from which they came. This exposed boroughs such as Erith, Bexley, and Crayford to more hits. For that they could blame the deceptions of the Double-Cross (XX) Committee, who directed the work of double agents and claimed they had induced the German army to shorten the range. The evidence for the claim is not strong, however. A week or two later, the MPI (Mean Point of Impact) south of the river went back to what it had been, so any deception, if there was one, must have been short-lived.

For the Bromley area, incident numbers are not sufficient for reliable analysis of this sort. The reader may notice, however, that for a time after January a greater proportion of local incidents took place in eastern parts of the area - at Sidcup, Chislehurst, Orpington, and St Mary Cray.

March 1945 started on a bad note, with Lancing Road, Orpington hit at 8.25am on the 1st (two killed and 57 injured); Rookesley Road, St Mary Cray hit at 4.52am on the 2nd (five killed, 46 injured); and Elm Grove/Orchard Grove, Orpington hit on the same day at 12.15pm (79 injured).

Another V2 came down at St Mary Cray on the 6th. This time ruining two acres of leeks on farmland at Sheepcote Lane/ Hockenden Wood. It was St Mary Cray again on the 8th at 4.35am. Rocket 961 blasted Station Square, injuring nine persons, and damaging the railway station, shops, houses, and factories. Rocket 966 came down that afternoon at Sidcup, in Marlborough Park Avenue, claiming two lives, injuring 17, and demolishing eight houses.

Beckenham and Biggin Hill were the targets on the 10th. At midnight, Marion Vian School was severely damaged by missile 981 at the rear of Shirley Crescent. Quarter of an hour later missile 982 blew up in a field near High House, Jewels Hill, about 600 yards from the RAF fighter station. Some damage was done to the officers' mess. On the 12th Rocket 998 blasted Bull Lane, Chislehurst at 2.35am, injuring five people. Red hot fragments from the missile destroyed the Working Men's Club by fire. Another fire burned down a house used for storing furniture. The NFS were unable to save the house because heavy furniture items had been blown about inside making access to the fire difficult, e.g., a piano completely jammed the front door shut.

A deafening explosion at dead of night shrouded by the impenetrable black out brought hundreds of people tumbling out of their beds, shivering in the chill air which poured through broken windows and doors forced open. They peered cautiously into the secretive gloom through the tattered remnants of curtains and shards of glass. Like as not, there was nothing to see. It had been near, but how near? And in which direction? Was it their business to go out in the cold, dark streets and see what had happened and give help? Should they phone the police or fire brigade? Surely *they* - the mysterious *they* - must know already what had happened. What were the wardens for, anyway? Best thing must be to sit quietly and wait for help to come.

Here among the large, upper middle class Victorian villas of Westwood Hill and Crystal Palace Park Road there was not a great deal of community spirit. Detached brick fortresses like these, set among extensive gardens and with no amenities within convenient walking distance, discouraged communal action. Privacy of spirit and withdrawal from one's fellows were accentuated by sub-letting of some houses to temporary, wartime tenants and to black out isolation, and to the fact that by about 10.30pm wartime London suburbs fell quite dead and deserted. All the same, it was a pity. Rocket 1,016 had exploded directly on 73-75 Crystal Palace Park Road at the junction of three districts - Beckenham, Lewisham, and Penge - and these were unsure of its exact location, hence of who was responsible for supplying the emergency services and taking charge. A phone call from a local resident might have saved much delay and confusion.

The time was 1am on 15 March 1945. Two four-storey villas had been demolished. Under the ruins in coldness and blackness, smothered and weighed down by tons of masonry and timber, an unknown number of injured, if still conscious, felt life slowly ebbing away in what must have seemed like the silent tomb of the forgotten and abandoned.

The location was, in fact, just feet inside Beckenham's border, the boundary line with Lewisham running down the middle of the road. Local wardens, who made two searches before finding the spot, incorrectly reported it as in Lewisham. Ambulance stations in Lewisham despatched eight ambulances, the first of which arrived thirty minutes after the blast. Beckenham failed to send any ambulances until 1.45am. These were then sent back without proper authority and later recalled to the incident.

Critical letters were exchanged between Beckenham and Civil Defence HQ about the handling of this incident, and Beckenham Controller was required to submit a full report. In it he complained that the warden service had been cut back, "... presumably on grounds of political expediency... and one cannot in these days have a guarantee of quick and accurate reporting". He insisted that Beckenham Control made repeated phone enquiries to confirm the location - to wardens' posts, the NFS, Catford and Gipsy Hill police stations, Penge and Lewisham Controls, etc. No one knew the answer. The first definite news was at 1.34am from Penge Control. No one was in the streets at the time, some residents slept through the explosion; no one phoned to report it, and Lewisham Control failed to keep Beckenham informed of what they knew or of what they were doing.

The Controller was right about the cutbacks. V2s offered less role for wardens: for they caused large, discrete incidents whose locations were usually detectable from fire station training towers. Mobile columns of NFS appliances, rescue parties, ambulances, paramedics, and support services typically converged on the spot without needing to be told by wardens reporting through control centres. Nevertheless, for the government to require sharp reductions in London's warden service while the rocket bombardment continued showed unseemly haste to reap in advance what we call today 'a peace dividend', with no regard for how much worse the attacks might become. Eight or nine bodies were recovered at the Crystal Palace Park Road incident, but because a depleted warden service no longer kept full records of house occupants the possibility of more could not be ruled out for some days.

At breakfast-time on 20 March, with streets busy with workers making their way to factories and offices, Sidcup was again the target. A huge spout of earth, a colossal crash, and an oven-hot wave of blast came together in a split second at Craybrooke Works in Craybrooke Road. The POI was in the builder's yard near the junction of Sidcup Hill and Sidcup High Street. Seven people died in a flash at Craybrooke Works. Two more lives were lost in the High Street and St John's Road. But scores of badly injured who had been queuing for buses in the High Street now lay moaning in the road or staggered around in a daze, streaming blood from head, face and body wounds. Queen Mary's Hospital was swamped by a stream of casualties brought in by a shuttle of ambulances. The injured totalled 98, of which over half were in a serious condition.

On the afternoon of 26 March, Raymond Wattenbach, still sticking it out at Bickley Hall School, was lining up with others in a long corridor before proceeding into the gymnasium to watch a boxing match, when came a sudden bang and loud crash of glass. Fortunately, he was not standing alongside any window but against a plain wall. The only person cut by falling glass was a boy named Jackson. "He was later carried past us presumably for treatment. He had been in the gym and it had a glass roof. The match was cancelled... I walked around outside and found a piece of metal which was still too hot to handle..."

The rocket (No. 1,107) had blown up in Tudor Close, Chislehurst, causing two deaths and eight injuries. Damage extended to the Bickley Arms (near the entrance to Chislehurst Caves), Christ Church, and Chislehurst station. A few hours later an undetected hot fragment of the rocket started a roof fire which spread and finally burned the house down.

The last salvo of Hitler's V2 rockets against England came on 27 March 1945. There was nothing to suggest to the average Londoner that this date would see the end of the ordeal. It was, indeed, another disastrous day for the capital at the hands of this futurist weapon from outer space. When dawn broke, four 'bolts from the blue' had already struck - Nos. 1,110 to 1,113 at Edmonton, Cheshunt, Ilford, and Brentwood. Then a malevolent fate delivered the penultimate missile on a block of flats in Stepney and claimed 134 lives and injured another hundred people, making the incident the second worst of the whole campaign for casualties, at the very moment light shone at the end of the tunnel.

It left only one more to come - rocket 1,115. This fell just before 5pm in rear gardens of Court Road and Kynaston Road, Orpington. Mrs Ivy Millichamp, at 88 Kynaston Road, was the sole person killed in the blast and the last civilian killed in Britain by enemy action in the Second World War. Someone had to suffer this cruellest cut of all, and it was the ill-fortune of an ordinary 34-year-old suburban housewife to be the one. The very first fatality had occurred five years earlier almost to the day on Orkney; 27-year-old James Isbister, killed in the village of Bridge of Waith. Orkney and Orpington being about as far apart as you can get in Britain, one might be forgiven for seeing a certain poignant symbol of the nationwide nature of air attacks on Britain in James Isbister's and Ivy Millichamp's deaths.

Mrs Millichamp's husband, Derek, was one of 56 people injured. He was not seriously hurt and was able to pull his wife out of the wreckage of their bungalow. He moved away from the neighbourhood not long afterwards and, like all the other bungalows destroyed or badly damaged, his home was re-built within six months. At 84 Kynaston Road, Mr and Mrs Moss were in their garden planting potatoes. She was closest of anyone to the V2. In fact, she was picked up off the lip of the huge crater made in the gardens. She heard nothing, but the blast bowled her over and bits of the rocket burned her. Other than this she was not seriously injured. Victor Moss, however, was badly hurt. An iron bolt from his workbench flew up and gashed his throat. The wound involved a month in hospital and several months' convalescence. He was still suffering from fainting spells five years later.

At No. 82, Mr and Mrs Hills, two pensioners, were in their kitchen preparing tea. Both were badly injured - the old man knocked senseless and his wife struck a severe blow on the head when the roof of their home blew off. Mr Hills recovered eventually, but his wife never got over it. She became bedridden, partially lost the sight of one eye, and spent long periods in

68) It was here near the corner of Craybrooke Road/ Sidcup High Street at breakfast time, 20 March 1945, that a V2 rocket exploded, causing nine deaths and nearly one hundred injured, among them early morning workers waiting at the bus stop shown. (Lewis Blake)

hospital. Detective Inspector Hine, at 69 Court Road, was in his favourite armchair listening to the radio, something about the war being virtually all over, when the house fell on top of him. Dazed under the wreckage, he wondered whether he was dead. He managed to wriggle out to find dust and smoke everywhere. When Mrs Hine came home from her war-time factory job, he was just standing vacantly in the ruins of their bungalow. They stayed with friends while their home was re-built. Compensation for their car, which was destroyed, was only £25, but the detective won £225 on the pools and bought another one. The V2 affected his nerves quite badly. Years later, sudden noises still caused him to jump up in alarm.

Evelyn Driscoll, aged 18 in 1945, told Jonathan Sale in the *Sunday Telegraph* 50 years later that she was pouring tea for her friend Daphne in her parents' home at 63 Court Road. "I happened to be facing the French window and I was hit by flying glass. It severed an artery in my temple and the blood ran into my eyes. I thought I'd been blinded." She passed out and woke up in hospital. Her face looked so horrific that the hospital would not let her look in a mirror, but she recovered and her skin healed. She never saw Daphne again. 50 years on she could not even recall her surname.

Rocket 1,115 in Orpington should have marked the end of German attacks in the Bromley area. It was not quite so. There was still the little matter of V1 flying bombs, which had started coming over again since 3 March from fixed launching sites in Holland. On that date Mrs Kennedy noted air raid sirens sounding at 3pm, "the first since 5 January", and she heard a Buzz Bomb in the distance.

Over the next four weeks 158 missiles were plotted by radar or the ROC. Not all reached the coast. Of those which did, AA guns shot down 88 and the RAF four. Only 13 reached the London area. One fell in Cudham Lane at 5.25am., 27 March, damaging Hostye Farm, Paddock Farm and houses known as Fairways and Granada. Finally, at 8am., 28 March, the sole survivor of a salvo of 16 flying bombs - 14 having been shot down and one falling harmlessly at Waltham Holy Cross - smashed into Scadbury Park, Chislehurst. Scadbury House was damaged and some outbuildings partially demolished. Fires burned down an iron and timber shed and a petrol store, and four people were seriously injured.

This was the last war-time incident in the Bromley area. It was also the last incident in Britain to cause casualties or material damage. The very last V1 on land was shot down by gunfire at Iwade, Sittingbourne next day, followed by the final shot of all within sight of the country - a V1 shot down by gunfire off Orfordness, Suffolk.

69 The last V2 rocket on British soil fell here at 4.57pm, 27 March 1945 - a lovely spring afternoon - in the rear gardens of Kynaston Road and Court Road, Orpington. Mrs Ivy Millichamp lost her life at 88 Kynaston Road and was the last British civilian to be killed by enemy action in the Second World War.

70) Scadbury House, Chislehurst. Scene of the last war-time incident in Britain to cause material damage and casualties when a V1 flying bomb exploded in the grounds, 8am, 28 March 1945. Scadbury House survived the war only to be destroyed in a fire, circa. 1980. (L. Blake)

CONCLUSION

No great sigh of relief went up in Bromley on 28 March 1945. Neither did people break out in celebration. Quite simply they had no way of telling that danger from the sky had passed. Only the end of hostilities in Europe on 8 May 1945 gave them that assurance. The condition of not knowing what the next day or hour held in store was fundamental to the civilians' situation. They never knew if their turn would be next.

Those with essential duties to carry out during attacks - Civil Defence, firefighters, hospital staff, police officers, train and bus crews, and many others - were probably kept too busy to dwell overmuch on the dangers they faced. Those whose only duty - and it was a duty - was to take cover had less to occupy their minds at times of maximum stress. Truly, they also served who sat and sheltered. Taking proper cover played a positive role in the war. Alive and uninjured, and getting adequate rest at night, civilians were assets in the struggle - keeping the fabric of society intact and fulfilling a myriad of tasks required in the fight. Hors de combat, whether through death or serious injury, they were no longer helping - hence the duty, albeit voluntary, to take proper shelter.

More subtly, perhaps, the simple act of drawing the enemy's fire helped the fighting directly by diverting enemy resources, especially air crews and aircraft, away from where they could be used against British forces. This the people did simply by doggedly refusing to crack under aerial assault, and by turning up at work benches, office desks, shop counters, food queues, kitchen stoves and sinks, even at school lessons, regularly each day.

From reading between the lines may be dimly perceived an amazing picture of fortitude and endurance of a civilian population carrying on their lives in the most trying of circumstances. It may be said that German civilians held out just as stoically under worse conditions. But it was London above all, including suburbs like Bromley, which gave the lead; which first demonstrated to the world that civilian morale need not break under persistent and heavy aerial attack, thereby silencing all the clever pundits who had argued otherwise. And they, along with the rest of the nation, did it without being coerced and intimidated into it by a secret police state.

APPENDIX

SUMMARY OF CIVILIAN CASUALTIES

DISTRICT	KILLED	INJURED (Appx)
Beckenham	362	1,800
Bromley	233	1,350
Chis & Sid	178	1,550
Orpington	141	1,000
Penge	104	750
Totals	1,018	6,450

Figures do not include residents killed or injured while outside the area, e.g., 26 Beckenham AFS killed in London's East End. Many cases of minor injuries would not appear in official returns.

CAUSES OF INCIDENTS BY TYPE
(Totals for Bromley area, including Sidcup)

HE Bombs	4,949 (includes 861 UXBs)
Parachute Mines	73
Oil Bombs	162
Incendiaries	65-70,000
PhIBs	125
VI Flying Bombs	249
V2 Rockets	45
Crashed GAF aircraft	20

(16 in Orpington district, which included Biggin Hill)

Miscellaneous	679 (e.g, AA shells, MG fire,etc)
Reported Incidents	5,075

(One incident might relate to many missiles, e.g, IBs)

Public Alerts	1,350 (Orpington)
	1,200 appx. other districts.

DAMAGE TO PRIVATE DWELLINGS

Homes Destroyed -	2,677
Homes Badly Damaged -	9,968
Total destroyed or badly damaged -	12,645
Total Housing Stock -	78,800

(16.1% destroyed or badly damaged. In Penge it was 42%. Almost all homes suffered some damage, perhaps on two or more occasions).

SOURCES & BIBLIOGRAPHY

Principal Sources

1) Public Record Office (now National Archives), Kew. In the main, Home Office/ Ministry of Home Security (HO) series; Air Ministry (AIR) series; and War Office (WO) series.

2) Commonwealth War Graves Commission's Roll of Honour, Civilian War Dead.

3) ARP Incident Books and a range of other documents, including local newspaper reports, -at Bromley Local Studies Library, Lewisham Local Studies Centre, Centre for Kentish Studies.

4) Fire reports, evacuation files, etc., at London Metropolitan Archives.

5) British Library, Newspaper Library, Colindale.

6) Guildhall Library, City of London.

7) Wide range of local histories of schools, churches, particular districts, etc., which almost invariably contain references to wartime events and conditions.

8) After The Battle Series, *The Blitz, Then And Now* (3 vols.)

9) Numerous private correspondents who have generously supplied personal memories, diaries, and documents of the times and concerning particular events.

Selected Local Works

Blake, Lewis *Red Alert - South East London, 1939-1945* The author, 1992

Blake, Lewis *Bolts From The Blue*. The author, 1990

Blake, Lewis *How We Went To War.* Lewisham Libraries, 1995

Boorman, H.R.P. *Hell's Corner*, Kent Messenger, 1942

Clarke, Helen *Modern Cave Dwellers*, The author, 1998

Cluett, Douglas; Bogle, Joanna and Learmouth, Bob *Croydon Airport and the Battle for Britain, 1939-1945.*

Creaton, Heather *Sources for the History of London, 1939-45* British Records Association, 1998

Gould, J.A., *History of the 19th County of London (South Suburban Gas Company) battalion, Home Guard,* South Suburban Gas Company, 1945

Holliss, Barry 37 *Fire Force (Fire and Rescue, South East London),* Enthusiasts Pub. 1988

London Evening News, *Hitler Passed This Way,* Associated Newspapers, 1945

London Fire & CD Authority, *Under Fire, The Blitz Remembered,* 1990

Ogley, Bob *Kent At War: the unconquered county, 1939-1945,* Frogletts/Kent Messenger, 1994

Redgrave, W.T., *Wardens Service In Bromley* Unpublished typescript in the Bromley Local Studies Collection, 1971

Rootes, Andrew *Front Line County: Kent at war, 1939-1945,* Robert Hale, 1988

Samways, Richard (Ed.), *We Think You Ought To Go, an account of the evacuation of children from London during the Second World War based on the original records of the London County Council,* Corporation of London, 1997.

Schweitzer, Pam *Goodnight Children, Everywhere memories of evacuation in World War II,* Age Exchange, 1990

Wilton, Eric *Centre Crew: a memory of the Royal Observer Corps, B Crew,* R.O.C. Bromley, 1946

Wright, Nicholas *The Bump,* RAF Biggin Hill, 1980.

Selected General Works

Bromley, Gordon *London Goes To War, 1939,* Michael Joseph, 1974

Collier, Basil *Defence of the United Kingdom,* H.M.S.O., 1957

Collier, Basil *The Battle of the V-Weapons, 1944-45* Hodder & Stoughton, 1964

Collier, Richard *The City that wouldn't die: May 10-11 1941,* Collins, 1959

Cooksley, Peter *Flying Bomb,* Robert Hale, 1979

Darwin, Bernard *War on the Line: the story of the Southern Railway in wartime,* Southern Railway, 1946

Deighton, Len *Battle of Britain,* Jonathan Cape, 1980

Dobinson, Colin *AA Command: Britain's anti-aircraft defences of World War II* Methuen, 2001

Firebrace, Sir Aylmer *Fire Service Memories,* Andrew Melrose, 1949

Graves, Charles, *London Transport At War 1939-1945,* Altmark, 1974

Harrisson, Tom *Living Through The Blitz*, Collins, 1976

Johnson, David *V For Vengeance*, William Kimber, 1981

Longmate, Norman *The real Dad's Army: the story of the Home Guard*, Hutchinson, 1974

Longmate, Norman *How We Lived Then: a history of everyday life during the Second World War*, Hutchinson, 1971

Longmate, Norman *Hitler's Rockets: the story of the V-2's*, Hutchinson, 1985

Morgan, Guy *Red Roses Every Night: an account of London cinemas under fire*, Quality Press, 1948

Nicholson, Mavis *What Did You Do In The War, Mummy? Women in World War II*, Chatto & Windus, 1985

Nock, O. S., *British Railways At War 1939-1945*, Ian Allan, 1971

O'Brien, Terence H., *Civil Defence*, HMSO, 1955

Pile, Gen. Sir Frederick, *Ack-ack*, Harrap, 1949

Price, Alfred *Blitz on Britain: the bomber attacks on the United Kingdom 1939-1945*, Ian Allen, 1977, reprinted Sutton Publishing, 2000

Titmuss, R. M., *Problems of Social Policy*, HMSO/Longmans, Green, 1950

Wallington, Neil *Firemen at War: the work of London's fire-fighters in the Second World War*, David & Charles, 1981

Winslow, T.E., *Forewarned is Forearmed*, Wm Hodge & Co, 1948

Wood, Derek *Attack Warning Red: the Royal Observer Corps and the defence of Britain 1925-1992*, Carmichael & Sweet, 1992

INDEX

N.B. Only major incidents are indexed here.
Other less serious ones may be found in the text.
Illustrations in bold

LIST OF ILLUSTRATIONS

1. Dornier 17 shot down off Blackness Lane, Leaves Green, 18 August 1940. (Imperial War Museum HU3122)
2. Biggin Hill air raid siren. (Lewis Blake)
3. 130 Lennard Road, Beckenham (Bromley Libraries D4/242)
4. Parklands Nursing Home, 19 Crystal Palace Park Road (Bromley Libraries C3/82)
5. The New Inn, Station Approach, Hayes. 15 September 1940. (Central Office of Information/Bromley Libraries H8/61)
6. Kenwood Court, Hayes Lane, Beckenham, 17 September 1940 (Bromley Libraries G5/92)
7. Effects of a parachute mine at Den Road, Shortlands, 19 October 1940. (Bromley Libraries G6/36)
8. One ton parachute mine on a naval quayside in 1940. (Lewis Blake)
9. Chislehurst Caves, interior (Chislehurst Caves)
10. Entrance to Chislehurst Caves (Lewis Blake)
11. Springhill AFS Fire Station (Author's collection)
12. 26 Johnson Road, Bromley Common (Bromley Libraries K6/13)
13. Merlin Grove, Eden Park (Bromley Libraries E6/37)
14. Gun Site on Hayes Common, Summer 1940 (Imperial War Museum H1386)
15. St. Christopher's Preparatory School, December 1940 (Bromley Libraries)
16. Searchlights at Night (Topfoto)
17. Carlton Parade, Orpington, March 1941 (Bromley Libraries Q6/182)
18. Mottingham Post Office, c1914 (Gus White/John Kennett Collection)
19. North Tower, Crystal Palace – demolition, 1941 (Corporation of London, London Metropolitan Archives)
20. Bromley Parish Church tower, 1941 (Lewis Blake)
21. Church House, Bromley c.1932 (Bromley Libraries H5/94)
22. Church House, Bromley, April 1941 (Bromley Libraries H5/95)
23. Central Hall, Bromley (Bromley Libraries H4/23)
24. 4 Park Hill Road, Shortlands (Bromley Libraries G5/70)
25. Bromley Market Square, April 1941 (Kent Messenger Group)
26. Churchfields Road, 1941 (Bromley Libraries)
27. Churchfields Road, 1980 (Lewis Blake)
28. St. Joseph's RC Church, St. Mary Cray, 2005 (Lewis Blake)
29. Map of incidents, 16-17 April 1941 (Lewis Blake)
30. Funeral of 19 Beckenham AFS (Empics/Sport and General)
31. Elmers End Station, 1941 (Bromley Libraries D6/98)
32. Warden's Post C3 Mason's Hill (W.T. Redgrave)
33. London May Queen 1941 (Kent Messenger Group)
34. Bromley war weapons week, 1941 (Bromley Libraries J5/851)

35. Bromley Salvage Drive, 1941 (Bromley Libraries J5/852)
36. NFS, Appliance at Biggin Hill Air Fair (Lewis Blake)
37. Home Guard/AFS Biggin Hill, 1942 (Bromley Libraries TOP 679/11)
38. Impression of FW190's over Bellingham (Lewis Blake)
39. Wreckage of JU88, behind Holy Trinity Convent, 1943 (S.A.J. Quilter)
40. Anglesea Road, St. Mary Cray (Bromley Libraries Q7/51)
41. Anglesea Road, 2005 (Lewis Blake)
42. Col. Chamberlain reviews 54th battalion Kent Home Guard, 1940 (Pictorial Illustrations/London Press Photos/Empics)
43. St Katherine's Church, Knockholt (Lewis Blake)
44. Holy Trinity Church, Penge (Bromley Libraries C5/13)
45. Rev. W.J. Berry, vicar of St. John's Eden Park (Sunday Graphic/NI Syndication)
46. St Michael and All Angels Church, 1944 (Estate of Rev. L. Smith/St Michael & All Angels Church)
47. V-1 Flying bomb (Author's Collection/Bexley Libraries)
48. Tylney Road, Bromley (Central Office of Information/Bromley Libraries K5/83)
49. West Wickham High Street, 1944 (Author's Collection)
50. Bickley and Widmore School (Harold White/Bromley Libraries K5/81)
51. Albemarle Road, Beckenham, July 1944 (Bromley Libraries F4/54)
52. Church Road, Beckenham, 1944 (Croydon Advertiser)
53. Beckenham Green, 2005 (Lewis Blake)
54. Elmers End Bus Garage, 1929 (London Transport Museum; copyright Transport for London/Bromley Libraries D5/106)
55. Elmers End Bus Garage, 1944 (London Transport Museum)
56. Beckenham Road, Beckenham, 1903 (Bromley Libraries D5/26)
57. Beckenham Road, Beckenham, August 1944 (Edward Davis/Bromley Libraries D5/22)
58. Beckenham Road, Beckenham, 2005 (Lewis Blake)
59. Hyde's Motor Works, Mottingham (F J Mott)
60. Mottingham Road Petrol Station, 2005 (Lewis Blake)
61. Lakes Road, Keston, 2005 (Lewis Blake)
62. V-2 Rocket (Author's Collection)
63. Southborough Lane, Bromley, 1944 (Lewis Blake)
64. Crooked Billet, Southborough Lane, Bromley (Bromley Libraries L6/10)
65. West Common Road, Hayes, 1945 (Author's Collection)
66. St John's Church, Eden Park (Author's Collection)
67. Christ Church, Beckenham, January 1945 (Bromley Libraries F5/208)
68. Sidcup High Street, 2005 (Lewis Blake)
69. Court Road, Orpington, March 1945 (Author's Collection)
70. Scadbury House, Chislehurst (Author's Collection)